USBORNE GUIDE TO
BIRDS
OF BRITAIN & EUROPE

ROB HUME

Contents

Introduction	3
Bird Key	4
Parts of a Bird	7
The Field Guide	8
Useful Addresses	126
Birdwatchers' Code	126
Index of English Names	127
Index of Scientific Names	128

Editorial Director Sue Jacquemier

Series Editor Rick Morris

Designer David Bennett

Researchers Patricia Monahan, Chris Parker, Jeff Cann

Illustrators Alan Harris, Trevor Boyer

Additional artwork by John Sibbick, Tony Murray, Mick Loates

A number of the illustrations in this book have been previously published in the Usborne Spotter's Guides series.

First published in 1981 by Usborne Publishing Limited, 20 Garrick Street, London WC2E 9BJ

© 1981 by Usborne Publishing Limited

Printed and bound in Great Britain by Fakenham Press Limited, Fakenham, Norfolk.

Introduction

This book is a guide to the identification of some of the birds of Britain and the rest of Europe, and is intended primarily for use in the field. The birds are grouped broadly into water birds, waterside birds and land birds, with similar-looking species and those of similar habitat placed near one another wherever possible. There is a key and a more detailed explanation of the way in which the birds in this book are grouped on pages 4-6.

The Illustrations

For each species, there is a large colour illustration of the bird, and further colour illustrations showing the most important variations of shape, size or plumage within the species (the male, female, immature or juvenile are included where necessary, as well as seasonal changes). The pencil drawings show a typical scene or habitat in which the bird might be found, and illustrates how the bird looks in the field; this sketch in many cases also illustrates a typical behaviour pattern. Some birds have distinctive display or escape flights and these are sometimes also illustrated.

When identifying a species, it can be misleading to rely solely on the illustrations: for example, a bird which looks like a Willow Warbler but which sings with a shivering trill will be a Wood Warbler; it is essential to read all the text in conjunction with the illustrations, in order to check that you have considered all the factors. It is best not to rely on any one feature as a basis for identification, and this book makes the task of checking all the features very simple, since they are all to be found on one page.

The Text

The main body of text underneath the illustrations gives details of the bird's size, the places in which it is likely to be found, the time of year when it can be seen in Britain, its nest-building and egg-laying habits, its calls, song or other noises, its feeding habits and distinctive features of its flight action. The text around the illustrations points out the main features of the species to aid recognition and includes comparisons with other species. There is a small introductory paragraph, usually next to the main colour illustration, which indicates the appearance, behaviour or other important features of the species; it also mentions species with which the bird might be confused or with which it can usefully be compared. In some cases, this point is so important as to require illustration; this can be found in a special panel at the top of the page, headed *Do not confuse.*

Measurements

Measurements are given in both metric and imperial terms, the metric figure being the nearest convenient estimate to the more accurate imperial figure. The sizes given refer to the length of the bird from the tip of its beak to the tip of its tail, when stretched out fully. Sometimes a range of sizes is given — these are cases in which the bird's size may vary from individual to individual.

The Selection of Species

The species illustrated include most of those likely to be seen in Britain by the average beginner. One or two species which are rare or not found in Britain are included because of their importance in other parts of Europe, and this is clearly stated in the text next to each bird. Birds that visit Britain either in the summer or winter may breed elsewhere, and in these cases no breeding details have been given in the text.

Bird Key

The birds in this book are grouped according to their appearance and habitat. This frequently coincides with the natural (scientific) family groupings, but occasionally these relationships have been over-ridden — hence the Fulmar is placed near the gulls (though not related to them), the wagtails are with the other birds of the riverside, and so on.

Nevertheless, it is useful to appreciate the true relationships of birds; it helps, for example, to know whether a bird is a duck or a grebe, or, at a more sophisticated level, whether a warbler is a Phylloscopus warbler or a Sylvia warbler. The latter distinction can be determined by studying the features of the birds in more detail, and by referring to the name of their genus (the first word in the bird's Latin name). The former distinction can be determined by using the key on the following pages.

How to Use the Key

To locate a bird in this book, first look at the illustrations in the key and read the accompanying description. When you think you have chosen the correct group, refer to the pages listed next to the relevant illustration. This will narrow down your choice to a few species, and final identification can then be made by checking the details of the bird's plumage, habitat, behaviour, etc. against the text and illustrations for that species.

Identifying Birds

This book provides the first step in helping you to identify birds, but nothing can replace experience when it comes to learning correct identification. It is advisable to learn the common birds first. When you know these really well, you will be much more able to tell when you have seen a less common bird. Note-taking trains you to look properly at birds; your notes will help you to distil the character of a species — known as its 'jizz' — the combination of colour, shape, action and other features which make each species recognisably unique.

SEABIRDS 8-11

Cormorants: large, dark, long-necked; slim, hooked bills; dive for food. *Auks:* penguin-like, upright on land; slender, low in water, expert divers. *Gannet:* Huge, long-winged, plunging for fish from air. See **Fulmar, gulls, terns.**

SWANS 12

Huge, white, long-necked, short-legged water birds; sexes alike, juveniles duller. Often in flocks; may be noisy in flight.

GEESE 13-15

Large, noisy water birds; heavier, more terrestrial than ducks. Often in spectacular flocks. Sexes alike.

DUCKS 16-25

Varied group of water birds, short-legged, long-necked, fast-flying. Surface-feeders dabble or up-end on water, or graze; diving ducks submerge to feed. Sexes usually differ greatly; also seasonal changes.

GREBES 26-27

Strictly water birds; expert divers, poor fliers. Slim necks often erect; bills more pointed than ducks ; almost tail-less. Do not fly in co-ordinated groups.

COOT, MOORHEN, WATER RAIL 28-30

Round-bodied, aquatic; *Coot* often in flocks on open water; *Moorhen* more restricted to water's edge, *Water Rail* to dense waterside vegetation. *Coot* dives for food, others pick or probe in wet places.

HERON 31

Huge, broad-winged, long-necked; neck erect or withdrawn. Seizes fish from shallows.

KINGFISHER 32

Small, highly-coloured but elusive; dives for fish from perch or hover. Large head and bill, tiny legs.

DIPPER 33

Unique shape, pattern and behaviour; favours shallow streams. Frequent springy bobbing.

WAGTAILS 34-35

Slender, terrestrial, strongly-patterned, with spindly legs. Long slim tails bobbed up and down. Loud calls in flight. Run and walk, sometimes in loose groups.

WADERS 36-48

Large, varied group of waterside birds. *Plovers:* short bills; tilt forwards to feed. *Sandpipers:* longer-billed; pick or probe for food from mud or sand, or wading in water. *Godwits* and *curlews:* much larger; long, straight or down-curved bills. *Snipe* and *Woodcock:* secretive, well camouflaged, very long-billed. Most smaller species are gregarious, sometimes flying in tight-knit, highly co-ordinated flocks. Calls and patterns revealed in flight are valuable for recognition. Walk and run.

GULLS 49-52

Medium to large waterside birds showing much white when adult. Expert fliers; also swim and walk readily. Colours of bill, legs and wing-tips provide useful clues when adult. Size, shape, plumage patterns and habitat always important. Noisy. Sexes alike but great variation according to age and season.

FULMAR 53

Superficially gull-like but large-headed, stiff-winged; heavy body merges into broad, less mobile tail; sea and cliff bird. Cannot walk.

TERNS 54-55

More slender, narrower-winged than gulls, with forked tails, pointed bills. Note colours of bill and legs. Often noisy and gregarious; not seen in winter.

BIRDS OF PREY 56-64

Varied group; medium to very large, with hooked bills, powerful feet. *Falcons:* slender, pointed wings set well forward, rapid wing-beats; perch upright. *Accipiters:* broader-winged, quite different in habitat and behaviour. *Harriers:* long legs, long wings and tails; fly slowly over ground. *Buzzards* and *eagles:* soar magnificently. *Osprey:* more like a huge gull. All are usually solitary or in family groups; perch for long periods; rarely walk far.

OWLS 65-67

Mostly nocturnal; large-headed, broad-winged, short-tailed predators with flat, disc-like faces.

GAMEBIRDS 68-70

Plump, round-bodied, mostly medium-sized, with small, round, chicken-like heads. Terrestrial; shuffling walk or sudden, noisy flight from cover, low, stiff and direct.

PIGEONS & DOVES 71-74

Medium-sized, plump, round-headed, fast-flying. Often in silent flocks in fields, taking flight with loud wing-noise but no flight calls. Crooning songs given from perch. Sexes alike.

CUCKOO 75

Medium-sized, slim, long-winged, broad-tailed, with slim, pointed head. Does not walk but drops to ground to feed.

WOODPECKERS, NUTHATCH, TREECREEPER 76-79

Woodpeckers: small to large, sharp-billed, stiff-tailed; cling upright to trees. Flight markedly undulating. Loud calls. *Nuthatch:* more agile, not using tail as support. *Treecreeper:* more unobtrusive, crawling upwards against bark.

SWIFT & HIRUNDINES 80-83

Aerial birds. *Swift:* never perches, all-dark. *Swallows* and *martins:* more flexible, often perch, strongly patterned. Long-winged, fork-tailed; tiny bills and feet.

LARKS & PIPITS 84-87

Terrestrial, small, streaky-brown. *Larks:* short crests, larger bodies than slender, narrow-tailed *pipits.* All walk or run; sing in air or from perch.

DUNNOCK 88

Unobtrusive, shuffling, streaky; slender bill.

WREN 89

Tiny, round, keeps to cover, often noisy.

CHATS 90-93

Chats and *allies:* small, variable, from the familiar Robin to boldly-patterned Wheatear. Upright, alert, often flicking wings and tail.

STARLING 94

Short-tailed, sharp-winged; greedy, bold and noisy; often in large, dense, bickering flocks.

THRUSHES 95-98

Larger, longer-tailed than chats; loud songs from perch; feed on ground; may form large, loose, quiet flocks.

WARBLERS 99-104

Small, active, insectivorous, often keeping in cover of foliage or reeds. Flit from perch to perch, not walking on ground. Mostly absent in winter. Note plumage pattern, song and calls.

FLYCATCHERS 105

Small, upright; make short, twisting flights after insects. Thin bill, short legs.

TITS 106-110

Bold, noisy, gregarious, often acrobatic. Actions less fluent than warblers'. Strikingly patterned; form mixed flocks but Marsh and Willow rarely in more than family groups. Flock behaviour not greatly co-ordinated.

GOLDCRESTS 111

Tiny, warbler-like but dumpier, with more tit-like actions. Frequent thin calls.

SPARROWS, FINCHES, BUNTINGS 112-119

Varied group; small, round-headed, stout-billed. Some feed on open ground or in fields, others in trees. *Sparrows:* noisy, often in flocks. *Chaffinch:* flocks are looser. *Smaller finches:* tighter, more co-ordinated groups. *Larger species* and *buntings:* more individual, less synchronised. *Buntings:* slimmer, longer-tailed than finches. All hop; sing from perch or in flight according to species.

CROWS 120-125

Black or boldly patterned. *Jay:* wary and often elusive. All gregarious (Rook especially so); strong, stout bills, strong legs; broad, blunt wings. Jaunty hop or plodding walk.

Parts of a Bird

These diagrams illustrate all the technical terms used in the text (and some additional ones) for the parts of a bird.

The terms *immature* and *juvenile* as used in this book refer to the non-adult plumages of birds. A juvenile is a bird which still has its first set of feathers, those which it had during its first flight on leaving the nest. At the first moult, some species go straight into the adult plumage; others moult into an immature plumage (there may be several such immature stages before full adult plumage is achieved).

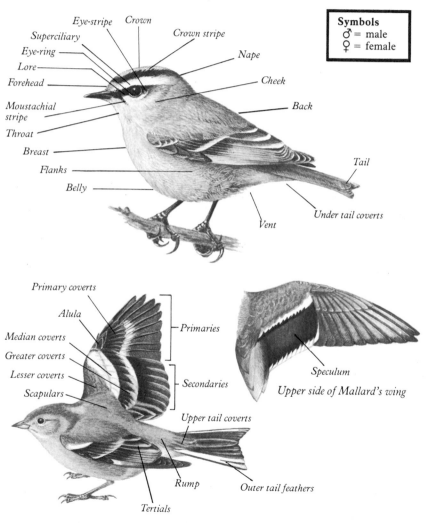

Symbols
♂ = male
♀ = female

Upper side of Mallard's wing

Parties high up often
fly in lines or in
V-formations

Neck is
extended

Tail is longer than
that of any goose

Cormorants often swim with their
bodies held very low in the water

Swims with bill
angled upwards

Browner
than adult,
with
white
underparts

White
chin
patch

IMMATURE

Back is browner
than Shag's

White thigh patch
in spring

Often perches
with open wings

Large, dark seabird with
long neck, broad tail and
stout body. Large white
chin patch; heavy head
and bill.

Cormorant

Phalacrocorax carbo 91cm/36"

Habitat: Quite varied – broad rivers, lakes, reservoirs and coastal waters, especially quiet estuaries and bays.

When seen: All year round.

Breeds: In colonies on cliff ledges on the coast; a few in trees. 3-4 eggs.

Voice: Deep, guttural croaks and grunts.

Feeding: Dives from surface for fish. Often brings large prey to surface.

Flight: Direct and fast with occasional glides. Often low over the sea but also higher.

Flies at a height less often than Cormorant

Broader-winged, longer-tailed and bigger than any duck in flight

A group on coastal rocks. The diving bird leaps clear of the water before submerging.

Crest only in early spring

Slender bill

Glossy green (looks black at a distance)

Yellow mark on gape

Small head

White chin-spot

Brown breast

Holds wings straighter than Cormorant when perched

IMMATURE

Sleek, dark seabird with no white marks. Slender, faster-flying and more agile then *Cormorant*, and with a smaller head and bill. Swims with bill uptilted like Cormorant.

Shag

Phalacrocorax aristotelis   76cm/30"

Habitat: More essentially maritime than Cormorant and often on rockier coasts.
When seen: All year round.
Breeds: In colonies on cliff ledges and in hollows and cavities. 3-4 eggs.
Voice: Harsh, guttural croaking and rattling alarm notes.
Feeding: Tends to leap clear of the water as it dives for fish.
Flight: Quicker action than Cormorant; rarely flies in large groups and usually flies very low over the water.

SUMMER

Pointed bill

Dark chocolate brown above (looks pale in strong sunlight)

Face and foreneck are white

WINTER

A cliff colony in summer

Superficially a penguin-like bird, standing upright on short legs, with a short tail. Swims with its bill horizontal and head raised.

SUMMER

Guillemot

Uria aalge   42cm/16½"
Habitat: Cliffs with ledges; flat-topped stacks; open sea.
When seen: All year round; at cliff sites from December to August.
Breeds: In colonies; lays one egg on bare rock on a cliff ledge.
Voice: Noisy at colonies – a variable, whirring or growling *aarrrr*.
Feeding: Feeds underwater, diving from the surface for fish and crustaceans.
Flight: Fast and direct with whirring wing-beats, poor manoeuvrability.

Glossy black above (never looks pale)

SUMMER

Stout bill has a white band and a white stripe to the eye

WINTER

Lower face and throat are white

A cliff colony

Similar to *Guillemot*, but has stouter, flat-sided bill and swims with pointed tail raised.

SUMMER

Razorbill

Alca torda   41cm/16"
Habitat: Like Guillemot, but also found on more broken cliffs, and on boulders; may be found higher up estuaries.
When seen: All year round; at sea in autumn and winter.
Breeds: In colonies, often with Guillemot; lays a single egg in a hole or crevice.
Voice: A whirring, grating *carrr*.
Feeding: Catches fish, crustaceans, and other small creatures underwater.
Flight: Low, fast and direct, like the Guillemot.

Pale grey face

Small, slender wings with stout head and body

Black upper parts

Brightly coloured, triangular bill

Brilliant vermilion legs and feet

SUMMER

Exceptionally attractive seabird. Winter birds, especially in flight or out at sea, can present problems, but breeding adults are unmistakeable.

Fish are held in a row across the bill

Puffin

Fratercula arctica   30cm/12"

Habitat: Open sea; nesting colonies on grassy slopes above cliffs, steep-sided islands.

When seen: At colonies from March to August; far out at sea in winter.

Breeds: In colonies; nests in natural holes or burrows into slopes; lays a single egg.

Voice: A low, repeated growling note – *arr*.

Feeding: Dives from the surface to take small fish underwater.

Flight: Fast and direct with quick, short wing-beats.

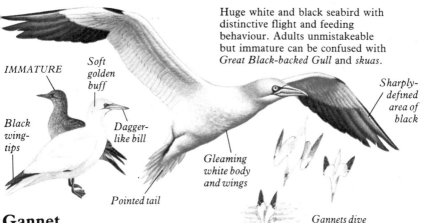

Huge white and black seabird with distinctive flight and feeding behaviour. Adults unmistakeable but immature can be confused with *Great Black-backed Gull* and *skuas.*

IMMATURE

Soft golden buff

Sharply-defined area of black

Black wing-tips

Dagger-like bill

Gleaming white body and wings

Pointed tail

Gannets dive vertically for fish

Gannet

Sula bassana   91cm/36"

Habitat: The open sea. Resorts to small, isolated islands, stacks or cliffs to breed; seen regularly close inshore near coasts adjacent to breeding sites.

When seen: All year round but scarce in winter.

Breeds: In large colonies on top of islands or stacks, or ledges on cliffs. One egg.

Voice: Harsh, deep, rhythmic calls at the colony.

Feeding: Catches fish by making a spectacular plunge from the air.

Flight: Steady, direct flight with regular wing-beats and lengthy glides.

Do not confuse with *other swans*

WHOOPER is same size as *Mute*

Flat forehead in profile

Large yellow patch extends forwards in a triangle

BEWICK'S is smaller than *Mute*

Rounded head

Smaller yellow patch is almost rounded

Both have loud bugling calls. Wings make little noise in flight.

A family of Mute Swans near the nest

Greyish bill with black base

Variably blotched grey-brown according to age

Head and neck are outstretched

IMMATURE

Black knob

Huge and white in flight with noisy wing-beats

Orange bill: no yellow

♂

Wings are arched in threat; otherwise flat against back

Familiar, huge, white water bird. Long neck is straight or curved, bill held downwards. Pointed tail is often angled upwards. Never has yellow on bill.

Pointed tail is often angled up

Mute Swan

Cygnus olor   152cm/60"

Habitat: Fresh water of all kinds, sheltered sea coasts.

When seen: All year round.

Breeds: Builds a massive nest near the water's edge. 5-8 eggs.

Voice: A variety of hissing and grunting noises; short, louder pitched calls, like a strangled, subdued bugling.

Feeding: Occasionally grazes on meadows but mostly feeds in shallow water, often submerging or 'upending'.

Flight: Strong, rapid flight but of limited manoeuvrability. Wing-beats produce a rhythmic, whistling hum. Head and neck are outstretched.

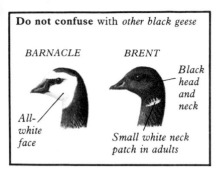

Do not confuse with *other black geese*

BARNACLE

BRENT

Black head and neck

All-white face

Small white neck patch in adults

Canada Geese on the shores of a lake

Black bill

White chin and face patch

Black neck

Pale breast

Brown back

Black tail and rump with white upper tail coverts

Black neck contrasts with pale belly

Black legs

Large, noisy, easily-identified goose. Pale breast with black neck and striking white face patch at all ages.

Canada Goose

Branta canadensis   91-101cm/36-40"
Habitat: Lakes, reservoirs, ornamental ponds, parkland.
When seen: All year round.
Breeds: A lined hollow in the ground near water, often on an island. 5-6 eggs.
Voice: Deep, loud, honking calls.
Feeding: Like a swan in shallow water or grazes on meadows like a grey goose.
Flight: Large groups fly in V-formation, in chevrons or loose flocks. Strong, fast flight, heavier than the smaller geese.

Often flies in loose, noisy lines

Rolls and tumbles before landing

Strikingly pale fore-wing

Pale rump

A flock of Greylag Geese grazing near fresh water

Heavy head

Plumage is pale greyish brown

Large orange bill with no black (see Pink-footed Goose)

Large, bulky goose, less agile than other grey geese. Pale overall, especially on head. Orange bill and pink legs.

Pale pink legs and feet

Greylag Goose

Anser anser 76-89cm/30-35"

Habitat: Freshwater areas (introduced birds), grassland, arable fields, estuaries.

When seen: All year round but most from September to April.

Breeds: Very small natural population in Scotland. Many more introduced elsewhere. 4-6 eggs in a lined hollow on the ground, near water.

Voice: A deeper chorus than other grey geese – loud, rattling, strident calls.

Feeding: Grazes on grass, stubble and in root fields during the day. Occasionally eats water weeds, sometimes 'up-ending'.

Flight: Strong and impressive. Large groups in V-formation or in chevrons.

14

White upper tail coverts

Head and neck held forward

Small, rounded head

Grey fore-wing

Black and pink bill

Large flocks fly in V-formation, in long lines or chevrons, or in more densely packed groups

Elegant, attractive goose. Dark head contrasts with pale chest and greyish back. Wild, nervous behaviour.

Pale chest

Pink legs

Pink-footed Goose

Anser brachyrhynchus 61-76cm/24-30"
Habitat: Marshes, estuaries. Flies inland to feed in fields during the day.
When seen: From September to April.
Voice: Flocks produce loud, babbling chorus of *ung-unk* calls. Higher *wink-wink* notes intermixed and more frequent from isolated birds.
Feeding: In stubble and root fields. Feeds like a farmyard goose but more agile.
Flight: Strong and direct. Rapid, aerobatic descent.

Slim wings

A boldly marked goose. Agile flight; active and noisy on ground. Can look strongly contrasted, dull, pale, dark, greyish or brownish, according to light conditions.

Moves slowly forward while pecking quickly to feed

Pink or orange bill: no black

White forehead (except on immatures)

Black barring

Striking orange legs are much brighter than on other geese

White-fronted Goose

Bold black barring on underparts (except on immature birds)

Anser albifrons 66-76cm/26-30"
Habitat: Wet pastureland, estuaries.
When seen: From October to April.
Voice: Flock chorus is higher pitched than other geese, with a ringing, laughing or yapping quality.
Feeding: Grazes on grassland in the daytime.
Flight: A little quicker and more dextrous than other geese, with rapid, twisting descent at times.

Do not confuse with *Gadwall*

♂

Mealy grey

Dark grey bill

White patch

Black stern

Broad, purple-blue speculum, edged with white

♂

♀

Mallards resting on a bank, upending and noisily splashing in the water

Areas of orange usually visible

♀

Mottled yellowish brown

Bright blue speculum (often concealed)

Short, whitish tail

Dark, glossy green head

♂

Pale bill

White neck-ring

White tail

Widespread, large dabbling duck. Male is very different from female except in summer 'eclipse' plumage.

Greyish body looks pale

Black stern

Mallard

Anas platyrhynchos   58cm/23"
Habitat: Fresh water of all kinds, quiet estuaries, marshes.
When seen: All year round.
Breeds: Nest is built in a hollow in the ground, in dense undergrowth or in a tree hole, and is lined with grass and down. 8-12 eggs.
Voice: Familiar loud *quack* (female only) and quieter, nasal calls.
Feeding: Surface-feeder; rarely dives. Often upends for vegetable and animal matter.
Flight: Fast, but heavier than smaller ducks; wings not lifted much above body level.

16

Do not confuse with *Garganey*

White stripe ♂

Pale flanks

Dark breast

Flocks twist in flight almost like groups of waders

♀

♂

Both sexes show brilliant green and black on white-edged speculum

Teal surface-feeding on a moorland pool; on take-off, they rise almost vertically from the water

Mottled greyish brown (see ♀ *Wigeon*)

Head is heavier than that of ♀ *Pintail*

Dark bill

Dark head

♀

♂

The smallest European duck. Quick and agile in flight. Much less tame than many *Mallards*; less terrestrial than *Wigeon*. Size, behaviour and generally dark appearance often more useful for recognition than pattern.

Yellowish patches surrounded by black

Black and white bands

Grey body often looks dark overall (see ♂ *Wigeon*)

Teal

Anas crecca 36cm/14"
Habitat: Reservoirs, lakes, marshes, estuaries, broad rivers.
When seen: All year round but most numerous from August to March.
Breeds: Concealed nest on ground near water, in lowland marshes and upland moors. 4-8 eggs.
Voice: Short *quack* and high-pitched, double ringing whistle *cric-cric*.
Feeding: Surface-feeder; 'dabbles' in shallows for seeds.
Flight: Very quick and active, capable of sudden dodging turns and dives.

Striking white fore-wing only in adult drake ♂

Pale fore-wing ♀

Pointed tail

Dark legs

Well-defined white belly is surrounded by darker colour (see ♀ Mallard)

Wigeon graze in noisy flocks on fields and marshes

Neat, rounded ducks, more terrestrial than most others and often seen grazing in large flocks. The small bill and round head are distinctive. Noisy and active; wild and shy.

Round head is brown or reddish

Dark brown body

Short grey bill ♀

Bright primrose-yellow forehead and crown ♂

Brown head contrasts with pale body (see Teal)

Black stern contrasts with white vent

White wing patch is often visible on pale grey body

Wigeon

Anas penelope   46cm/18"

Habitat: Floodmeadows, marshes, lakes and reservoirs; saltmarshes.

When seen: From August to April; a few remain to breed.

Breeds: Nest is a depression in the ground, lined with grass and is well concealed, close to a lake or marsh. 6-10 eggs.

Voice: A harsh growl and a loud, explosive whistle *whee-ooo*.

Feeding: Mostly grazes on vegetable matter from meadows and marshland.

Flight: Rapid and very manoeuvrable. Forms large, dense flocks.

Shorter wing and neck than surface-feeders; longer-winged than Tufted Duck

Both sexes have dark wings with a paler grey central bar

Pale belly and under-wing

Colourful, rather inactive diving duck, showing less plumage variation than many species. Often associates with *Tufted Duck*. Behaviour is completely different from the superficially similar *Wigeon* and *Teal*.

Brown head with pale area around bill, eye and chin

A flock of Pochards, with two birds pattering over the water before take-off

Dull, greyish body

Dark bill with pale panel

Chestnut-red head, red eye

Black breast contrasts with pale grey body

Black stern

Pochard

Aythya ferina 46cm/18″
Habitat: Open fresh water, lakes and reservoirs.
When seen: All year round.
Breeds: In dense vegetation such as reeds, beside quiet freshwater lakes.
Voice: Harsh flight call; nasal, wheezy display note.
Feeding: Dives from surface to take vegetable matter from under the water. Feeds mostly at night; sleeps during the day.
Flight: Direct and fast, less agile than surface-feeding ducks.

Very long neck and bill make wings look set far back ♂

♀

Bright, pale blue fore-wings in both sexes (see Mallard)

Feeding Shovelers swim with hunched shoulders and the head held low with most of the bill submerged

Mottled brown plumage (similar to ♀ Mallard's)

♀ Large grey bill with orange sides

Green-black head

♂

Large bill

Rather large surface-feeding duck with a long heavy bill. Swims with head low and forepart of body often almost awash. Male is similar to female in eclipse.

Chestnut flanks contrast with white breast (but see Shelduck)

Bright white breast

Shoveler

Anas clypeata   *51cm/20"*
Habitat: Lakes, reservoirs, flooded gravel pits, marshes.
When seen: All year round.
Breeds: In a shallow, lined hollow, hidden in vegetation near water. 8-12 eggs.
Voice: A quiet bird; low *quacks*, similar to Mallard, but quieter.
Feeding: Sieves vegetable and invertebrate food from water surface using huge bill.
Flight: Similar to Mallard. Wings make a characteristic *woofing* noise.

20

The most elegant of the surface-feeding ducks. Has short legs, a slender body, long slim neck and slim bill. Wild, much less common than *Mallard*.

Long thin neck ♂

Slim grey bill ♀

Pointed tail

Paler, greyer than Mallard

Grey and black bill ♀

Pale trailing edge

Long black tail

♂

White stripe

Black stern

White breast

Grey body

White breast

Pintail

A group of Pintails feeding

Anas acuta   56cm/22″
Habitat: Estuaries, saltmarshes and floodmeadows.
When seen: From September to March; a few stay to breed.
Breeds: In a lined hollow on the ground near a lake or floodmeadow. 7-10 eggs.
Voice: Very quiet for a duck. Gives on occasional *quack*.
Feeding: Largely at night. Takes vegetable and invertebrate food from water.
Flight: Swift and direct with outstretched head and rapid wing-beats.

Large, heavy, placid maritime duck. Long, flat head profile is very distinctive. Immature males may show all sorts of transitional stages.

♀

♂

Green neck markings

Buff-brown or grey-brown bars

A group of Eiders by the seashore

♂

Bright pink breast

♂

IMMATURE

Eider

Black underparts

Somateria mollissima   58cm/23″
Habitat: A sea-duck, rarely inland. Found off rocky coasts and in wide sandy bays.
When seen: All year round.
Breeds: In loose colonies amongst rocks or vegetation near the shore. 4-6 eggs.
Voice: Loud, throaty calls and various pleasing, smooth, crooning notes.
Feeding: Dives from surface to eat mussels and other shellfish, crustaceans, etc.
Flight: Often low over the waves, usually in a line; steady and direct.

Do not confuse with *Scaup*

Grey back | No crest | Broad bill

♂

Larger and bulkier than *Tufted Duck* with more rounded head. Female *Scaup* has large patch of white around the bill.

Rounded, dumpy birds in flight

Tufted Ducks often feed in groups. The ♀ in the foreground has a white area around the bill – this is smaller and less bright than in the ♀ Scaup

White wing-bar is obvious in both sexes

♀

Striking white belly

♂

Yellow eye

Grey bill

Thin, drooping crest

Round head

♀

Grey bill

Dark brown, with very little pattern

♂

Sometimes has white under-tail

Dumpy, active diving duck often in large parties. Rounder bodied, with tail usually less cocked than surface-feeding ducks.

Body is distinctively black and white, even at a distance

Tufted Duck

Aythya fuligula 43cm/17"
Habitat: Freshwater lakes, reservoirs, rivers, park ponds.
When seen: All year round.
Breeds: In dense vegetation on ground close to lakes. 8-11 eggs.
Voice: Harsh growling flight call. Musical, soft whistling display notes.
Feeding: Submerges from surface to take animal and vegetable matter.
Flight: Fast and direct, like Pochard, forming irregular flocks.

Blunt, straight wings

♂

White neck and belly

Display posture

Patters on water to take off

Large, rounded head (see Goosander)

♀

Whole groups of Goldeneyes sometimes dive together; males and females are often in separate groups

Large white wing patches (see Goosander, Great Crested Grebe)

Domed brown head

Often looks very dark – white on neck and wings is often hidden at rest

Conspicuous yellow eye

Small dark bill

♀

Green head appears black

Large white face spot

Thin, drooping black lines

A lively duck, and an expert diver. Has a short bill and a large head with a peaked crown. The tail is sometimes cocked and is rather long and pointed. Easily confused with Tufted Duck at a distance.

♂

Body is brilliant white, without grey or pink (see Goosander)

Goldeneye

Bucephala clangula   46cm/18″
Habitat: Sheltered coastal waters, open lakes and reservoirs, moorland pools.
When seen: From October to April.
Voice: Silent except for a nasal, grating display call.
Feeding: Dives from the surface to take crustaceans underwater.
Flight: Quick and agile with whistling wing-beats. Parties form an irregular flock and rapidly gain height.

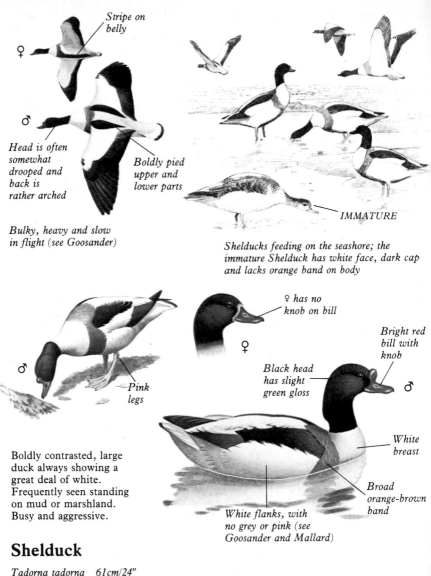

Stripe on belly

♀

♂

Head is often somewhat drooped and back is rather arched

Boldly pied upper and lower parts

Bulky, heavy and slow in flight (see Goosander)

IMMATURE

Shelducks feeding on the seashore; the immature Shelduck has white face, dark cap and lacks orange band on body

♂

Pink legs

♀ has no knob on bill

♀

Black head has slight green gloss

Bright red bill with knob

♂

White breast

Boldly contrasted, large duck always showing a great deal of white. Frequently seen standing on mud or marshland. Busy and aggressive.

Broad orange-brown band

White flanks, with no grey or pink (see Goosander and Mallard)

Shelduck

Tadorna tadorna   61cm/24"
Habitat: Sandy coasts, dunes, estuaries, mudflats, large inland lakes.
When seen: All year round.
Breeds: Usually in a hole in the ground or under dense thickets. 8-10 eggs.
Voice: Rhythmic, deep, *gah-gah-gah* and whistling notes.
Feeding: Grazes on marshes and mudflats but also dabbles in water.
Flight: Strong direct flight with wings flapped below body level.

Like *Goosander*, a long-bodied, slender-billed duck. Both look about the size of *Mallard* but slimmer, with tail depressed when swimming.

Wispy crest ♀

Slender head and neck ♀

♂

Orange legs

Wispy crest ♂ *Red bill*

White collar

Dull brownish grey

Grey flanks

Brownish breast

Red-breasted Merganser

A flock of Mergansers on the sea

Mergus serrator   58cm/23"
Habitat: Sea coasts. Some on lakes and rivers in breeding season.
When seen: All year round, but mainly from September to April.
Breeds: A few in the North and West. Nests on the ground near water. 8-10 eggs.
Voice: A harsh *karrr*.
Feeding: Dives expertly from the water surface for fish.
Flight: Fast, direct and low; has a very elongated profile.

Similar to *Red-breasted Merganser*, but male has no grey on body, and has white breast. Female Goosander has white chin (more sharply defined than in female *Merganser*) and paler grey body.

White on wings (both sexes)

♂

♀

Orange legs

Chestnut head ♀

Drooped mane

White throat

Dark red bill ♂

White breast

Pale body with pink flush

Goosander

Goosanders are regularly seen on ground beside water

Mergus merganser   66cm/26"
Habitat: Lakes and rivers (with wooded banks in breeding season), reservoirs.
When seen: All year round.
Breeds: In the North and West; 8-11 eggs in a tree-hole near water.
Voice, Feeding and Flight: Like Red-breasted Merganser.

Trailing legs

SUMMER

Large white wing patches (see Goosander)

Head is extended and drooped

Slim, long-necked, elegant waterbird. Neck is often retracted but looks long when held erect. Legs are set far back; very rarely seen on land. Neck and breast are satiny-white.

♂ and ♀ with striped chicks, which are often carried on the parent's back

SUMMER

Black head tufts

Chestnut frill

WINTER

Black crown

White face and neck

Grey-brown or blackish back

Silvery flanks

Brilliant white chest

Pointed, slender bill shows pink at close range

Great Crested Grebe

Podiceps cristatus   48cm/19"
Habitat: Large, reed-fringed lakes, reservoirs; open water with flooded willows etc. at edge; less often on big rivers. Regularly on the sea, especially in winter.
When seen: All year round.
Breeds: Amongst reeds, willows or other flooded or floating vegetation. 3-4 eggs.
Voice: Loud, throaty growls in summer. Young birds have high pitched whistling notes.
Feeding: Dives expertly from surface to catch fish, tadpoles, etc.
Flight: Rapid, direct, with poor manoeuvrability. Fast wing-beats.

SUMMER

Short weak wings

Trailing legs

JUVENILE

Small, round, tail-less diving bird. Dumpier than ducks, with blunter tail-end and short, pointed bill. Legs are set far back. Essentially dull brown in winter, brown and black in summer.

The nest is anchored to aquatic plants and the eggs are covered in the bird's absence; the juvenile has a striped head

Dark crown

Appears mainly dull brown

Fluffy, whitish tail-end

Short, pointed bill

Pale cheek

Bright, red-brown cheeks

WINTER

Pale spot

SUMMER

Appears mainly brown and black

Little Grebe

Tachybaptus ruficollis   27cm/10½"
Habitat: Lakes, reservoirs with well-vegetated margins; ponds, rivers.
When seen: All year round.
Breeds: Nest is a platform or large heap of damp vegetation. 4-6 eggs.
Voice: A drawn-out, whinnying trill in spring and summer.
Feeding: Eats small fish and amphibians caught underwater. Dives repeatedly.
Flight: Scutters across water surface; rarely seen in prolonged flight. Weak flight action, with rapid wing-beats.

Legs trail
in flight

Shape is more
rounded than that of
juvenile Moorhen

Tail is
never
raised

A large flock of Coots on a lake;
the white frontal shields are
visible from quite a distance

Whitish face
and breast

JUVENILE

Body is greyer than
head; plumage looks black
at a distance, with no
white markings

White frontal
shield and
white bill

Larger and heavier than
Moorhen, more often on
open water. More upright
and a rounder shape on
land. White frontal shield
and bill are diagnostic.

Large
lobed
feet

Coot

Fulica atra   38cm/15"
Habitat: Large areas of fresh water with reeds, etc. on shores; open grassy banks.
When seen: All year round.
Breeds: 4-8 eggs in a large nest in shallow water – sometimes a huge heap of vegetation.
Voice: Loud, metallic single or double notes – *kowk, kekowk*, etc.
Feeding: Dives from surface for vegetation; also feeds in groups on open shoreline.
Flight: Quite weak – often merely a scuttering across water surface; sometimes quite
high with head extended, quick wing-beats.

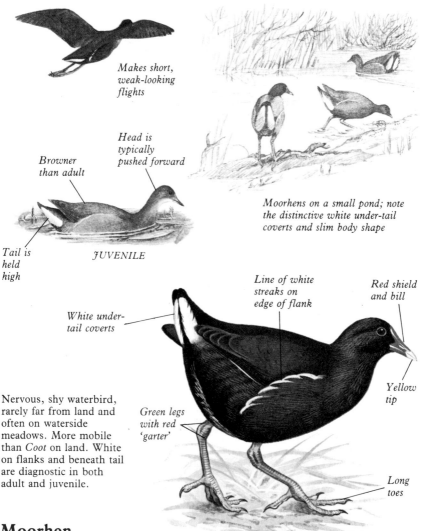

Makes short, weak-looking flights

Head is typically pushed forward

Browner than adult

JUVENILE

Tail is held high

Moorhens on a small pond; note the distinctive white under-tail coverts and slim body shape

Line of white streaks on edge of flank

Red shield and bill

White under-tail coverts

Yellow tip

Nervous, shy waterbird, rarely far from land and often on waterside meadows. More mobile than *Coot* on land. White on flanks and beneath tail are diagnostic in both adult and juvenile.

Green legs with red 'garter'

Long toes

Moorhen

Gallinula chloropus   33cm/13"
Habitat: Small ponds, lakes, marshes and slow streams.
When seen: All year round.
Breeds: 5-11 eggs in a nest amongst shoreline vegetation or branches touching water.
Voice: A variety of loud, explosive calls – *kittik, kurruk,* etc. and quieter calls.
Feeding: In shallow water or on muddy or grassy areas; takes seeds, fruit and other vegetable matter, insects, tadpoles, etc.
Flight: Scutters across water; longer flights usually low and fast but weak-looking.

Trailing legs
in flight

View of
bird
fluttering
away

Buff under-tail
coverts are visible
as bird runs
for cover

Water Rails skulking in the reeds; they
like plenty of thick waterside cover

Smoky-grey
face and
breast

Warm brown upper
parts with
dark streaks

Slender bill,
usually showing
a lot of red

Secretive, skulking bird,
often hard to see in dense
vegetation. Exceptionally
slim when seen end-on,
but from side tends to look
round with cocked tail and
long bill. Has a more
elongated shape when alert.

Black and
white bars on
flanks (see
Moorhen)

Water Rail

Rallus aquaticus   28cm/11"
Habitat: Reedbeds, overgrown ditches, well vegetated riversides, etc.
When seen: All year round, but commoner in winter in most areas. A sparse nesting bir
Breeds: Small, well hidden nest often slightly raised in reeds, etc. 6-11 eggs.
Voice: Heard more than seen; sharp *kik, kik* and various piglet-like squeaking sounds.
Feeding: Takes a variety of animal and vegetable matter, sometimes even small birds,
chicks and eggs. Comes into the open on muddy areas when undisturbed.
Flight: Prefers to run for cover; flight is quick and direct.

Head and neck are withdrawn in flight

Trailing legs

Broad, rounded downcurved wings

Heron standing on one leg beside a ditch, its head hunched into its body

White head with black stripe and crest

Greyish head and neck

IMMATURE

Grey body

Dagger-like bill is brownish or yellowish, but pink or orange in spring

Black shoulder patch

Black on belly

Very large, grey waterside bird. Often inactive, beside water, a ditch or even in a dry field. May be seen hunched (but upright) or with slender neck erect.

Grey Heron

Ardea cinerea   91cm/36"
Habitat: Edges of water and marshes of all kinds, fresh and salt.
When seen: All year round.
Breeds: In colonies. Huge stick nest is usually built in a tree. 4-5 eggs.
Voice: Typically a loud, strident *fraank*. Is noisy at nest.
Feeding: Catches fish, frogs, rats, etc. in and around shallow water.
Flight: A majestic flier around the colony, and surprisingly acrobatic. Direct flight is typically slower with distinctively arched wings.

Brilliant blue streak running down back

Typical hovering position before diving

Typical view of a Kingfisher perched on a low branch over a river

Stout bill is 4cm/1½" long

White throat patch

White neck patch

Warm, chestnut-orange underparts

Brilliant blue back

Wings are greener than back

A very shy bird, often glimpsed only as a bright flash of blue and green. The shrill whistle helps to locate it before it is seen – especially in flight.

Short tail

Kingfisher

Alcedo atthis   16.5cm/6½"
Habitat: Clean, fresh water of all kinds; seashores in winter.
When seen: All year round.
Breeds: Excavates a long tunnel in the vertical bank of a stream or sand-bank.
2 broods. 6-7 eggs. Nest-hole is often betrayed by droppings.
Voice: The loud, shrill whistle draws attention to an otherwise inconspicuous bird –
keee, chi-kee, kikikik-ik-keee, etc. Song is trilling, even warbling.
Feeding: Dives from a low perch or hovers into clear water for small fish, tadpoles, etc.
Flight: Fast and low over water; swings out across fields to avoid people on river bank.
May fly higher over land or amongst tall trees during spring courtship.

Flies fast and low over surface of water

Translucent membrane, which protects the eye; the bird also has a bright white eyelid

Dippers feeding in a rocky stream; they often bob up and down while standing on boulders

Short tail

Brown head

BRITAIN & C. EUROPE

N. EUROPE, IRELAND & S.W. EUROPE

Pure white gorget

Brown belly

Black belly

A rounded, short-billed, stout-legged bird, never found away from water. White breast is diagnostic. Whole body bobs up and down as legs are rhythmically flexed, especially when alarmed.

Dipper

Cinclus cinclus   18cm/7"

Habitat: Clear streams, rapid rivers with tree-lined banks and boulder-strewn shores, edges of lakes in hills; lowland rivers, lakes and sea coasts in winter.

When seen: All year round.

Breeds: An untidy domed or roofed nest always very close to water. Usually 5 eggs.

Voice: Sudden, loud *zit zit* calls. Frequent song by both sexes practically all year round consists of loud warbling with sweet and harsh notes intermixed.

Feeding: Can wade, swim, dive from the air or water surface; can also walk along river bottoms searching for aquatic insects, tadpoles, tiny fish, etc.

Flight: Fast, direct and low along the course of even the most twisting streams.

♂ PIED

♂ WHITE

♀ Pied Wagtail is greyer and more like a ♂ White Wagtail

Wagtail in a car park after rain

Bounding flight, with shallow undulations; bursts of wing-beats between short glides with wings closed

Yellowish face and throat

Grey upper parts

Dark breast patch

JUVENILE PIED or WHITE

White face

Upper parts are black or sooty

Blackish rump

Black bib

♂ PIED WAGTAIL (BRITAIN)

Black cap is isolated from black bib

♂ WHITE WAGTAIL (EUROPE)

Grey rump

Browner on wings than Pied Wagtail

Pale flanks

These are two forms of the same species. The Pied is found in Britain, the White in the rest of Europe. The wagtails' distinctive up-and-down bobbing of the tail is especially evident in this species.

Pied and White Wagtails

Motacilla alba   18cm/7"

Habitat: Open country varying from grassland to urban areas. Usually near water. Roosts in reedbeds, roadside trees, buildings in cities.

When seen: All year round; White Wagtail is a passage migrant in Britain.

Breeds: Nest is built in a hole, on a ledge, etc. in a variety of sites. 5-6 eggs.

Voice: A tuneless *tchissik;* a loud musical *tchuwee;* infrequent twittering song.

Feeding: Takes insects from the ground, often after a short lunge or dash, or from the air, in short flycatching sallies.

Flight: Typical buoyant wagtail flight with bounding undulations.

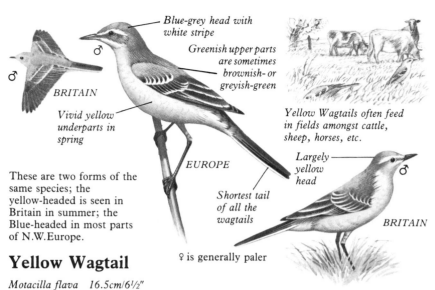

Blue-grey head with white stripe

Greenish upper parts are sometimes brownish- or greyish-green

BRITAIN

Vivid yellow underparts in spring

Yellow Wagtails often feed in fields amongst cattle, sheep, horses, etc.

EUROPE

Largely yellow head

Shortest tail of all the wagtails

These are two forms of the same species; the yellow-headed is seen in Britain in summer; the Blue-headed in most parts of N.W.Europe.

BRITAIN

Yellow Wagtail

♀ is generally paler

Motacilla flava   16.5cm/6½"
Habitat: Watermeadows, marshes, farmland; beside lakes and reservoirs.
When seen: Usually from April to late September; absent in winter.
Breeds: Nest is in a hollow on the ground, well hidden. 5-6 eggs. Often 2 broods.
Voice: Usually a shrill, explosive *tsweep;* a simple warbling song with calls intermixed.
Feeding and Flight: Like Pied Wagtail.

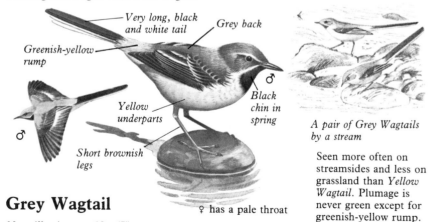

Very long, black and white tail

Grey back

Greenish-yellow rump

Yellow underparts

Black chin in spring

Short brownish legs

A pair of Grey Wagtails by a stream

Seen more often on streamsides and less on grassland than *Yellow Wagtail.* Plumage is never green except for greenish-yellow rump.

Grey Wagtail

♀ has a pale throat

Motacilla cinerea   18cm/7"
Habitat: By water, such as rocky streams; the coast, even urban areas, in winter.
When seen: All year round, unlike Yellow Wagtail.
Breeds: Builds nest amongst tree-roots in stream banks, in cavities in cliffs or walls, usually close to a stream. 4-6 eggs. Often 2 broods.
Voice: Higher pitched than Pied Wagtail – *tchick* or *tsisik;* warbling, twittering song.
Feeding and Flight: Like Pied Wagtail.

Large flocks form irregular masses flashing black and white

Common posture on landing

Black band

White rump

Broad, rounded wings

Long, wispy crest

Lapwings with a young chick on farmland

Upper parts are iridescent green with bronze and purple reflections on bend of wing

Short black bill

Black, white and buff face

Black breast-band contrasts with white underparts

Distinctive shape, bold pattern and voice make the Lapwing easy to identify. Upswept crest is obvious on ground; broad wings are characteristic in flight. Often forms large flocks.

Lapwing

Vanellus vanellus   30cm/12"
Habitat: Arable lands, pastures, moorland, watermeadows; lakes and coasts in winter.
When seen: All year round, but scarce in many lowland and coastal areas in summer.
Breeds: Grassy nest on open ground, often on a slight mound. Usually 4 eggs.
Voice: A wheezy *pee-weet*. Display flight song is a nasal *peer-weet-weet-weet*.
Feeding: Takes insects, worms, etc. from the ground in typical methodical plover way, pausing every few feet to tilt forward to pick up food.
Flight: Slow wing-beats and steady direct flight over distances; shorter flights may be more wavering. Display flight involves twisting plunges, low flight across ground.

Pointed, angled wings

Spangled yellow, black and white above

Winter birds in a field

Pale wing-bar

Variable amount of black on belly

WINTER

S. EUROPE SUMMER

N. EUROPE SUMMER

Typical plover with round head, short bill and rounded body that can look either dumpy or slim.

Golden Plover

Pluvialis apricaria 28cm/11"
Habitat: High moorland; pastures, arable land, coasts in winter.
When seen: All year round, but chiefly in lowland areas in winter.
Breeds: Nests in a scrape on the ground. Usually 4 eggs.
Voice: A high, whistling *tlui*. Trilling song.
Feeding: Takes insects, molluscs, worms, seeds, etc. from the ground.
Flight: Fast and agile, often in huge packs or V-formations.

WINTER

Striking black face and underparts

Black 'armpit' patch

Whitish wing-bar

White rump

WINTER

Blue-grey upper parts

Heavy black bill

SUMMER

Large dark eye

WINTER

Winter birds on the shoreline

Similar to *Golden Plover*, but more grey and looks larger, with a bigger bill. Black 'armpits' are diagnostic.

Grey Plover

Pluvialis squatarola 28cm/11"
Habitat: Usually sandy shores or muddy estuaries in the British Isles.
When seen: Mostly a winter visitor or a passage migrant.
Voice: Highly distinctive trisyllabic whistle – *tlee-oo-ee* – with middle note lower.
Feeding and Flight: Like Golden Plover, but usually flies in small groups.

Do not confuse with *Little Ringed Plover*

Dark bill

Pinkish-yellow legs

No obvious wing-bar

Summer visitor, smaller and more often inland than *Ringed Plover;* call is an abrupt *pew.*

White patches show in flight

SUMMER

Broad white wing-bar

SUMMER

No black on head

JUVENILE

Compare black-tipped orange bill of adult with dark bill of juvenile

SUMMER

Orange legs (may be soiled by mud)

Ringed Plovers looking for food on a shingly shore; they pause between short runs to tilt their whole body over and seize their prey

Bold black and white marks on head; in winter adult's head looks more like juvenile's

Widespread, distinctively-marked shorebird, often seen near water's edge. In flight, white wing-bar distinguishes it from *Little Ringed Plover.*

Ringed Plover

Charadrius hiaticula 19cm/7½″
Habitat: Sandy or muddy coasts; often beside freshwater areas inland.
When seen: All year round.
Breeds: Nest is a shallow depression, sometimes lined with stones, pieces of shell, on beaches, dunes, saltmarshes. Usually 4 eggs.
Voice: *Too-li* or *coo-eep*, rich and fluty. Song is a tremulous, prolonged, slow trill.
Feeding: Takes small molluscs, crustaceans and insects from shore.
Flight: Rapid, with regular wing-beats; generally low down.

Flickering patches and stripes of white are visible in flight

WINTER

SUMMER

SUMMER

Piebald head and neck

SUMMER

Stout, slightly upcurved bill

Broad black breast-band

WINTER

Bright orange or vermilion legs in all seasons

A group of winter birds feeding on seaweed-covered rocks amongst waves; they fly low over the sea and shore when disturbed

Black and glossy chestnut pattern on upper parts

Upper parts are duller and darker in winter

Stout, short-legged shoreline wader. Habitat and behaviour are distinctive; pulls seaweed and overturns stones with its bill as it seeks food.

Turnstone

Arenaria interpres 23cm/9"

Habitat: Typically stony or rocky coasts with a lot of seaweed; also sandy or muddy shores with rocks and mussel-beds.

When seen: All year round on coasts, but most numerous in winter.

Voice: Short, sharp notes run together as a staccato chatter or trill – *tuc-a-tuc, kitititit,* etc. Lower pitched and less piping than chatterings of Oystercatcher.

Feeding: Takes molluscs, crustaceans, insects, etc. from amongst seaweed and stones.

Flight: Usually low and fairly fast; often separates from Dunlins etc. when flushed.

Flying birds in winter show dark upper sides and white undersides when they twist and turn as a flock

SUMMER

White sides to tail and rump

SUMMER

Pointed wings are dark with a long white stripe

Winter birds feeding; their actions are slower than Sanderlings', and without the distinctive tilting action of the plovers

Medium-length bill is slightly down-curved (see Sanderling)

WINTER

Mousy-brown upper parts, white below

Variable amount of chestnut on upper parts

Small, round-shouldered, short-necked wader, very variable in plumage but its shape, behaviour and call remain characteristic. Black belly patch, medium-length bill and chestnut upper side are diagnostic in summer.

SUMMER

Black belly patch

Dunlin

Calidris alpina   18cm/7"
Habitat: Muddy estuaries, saltmarshes, rocky shores, sandy beaches; breeds on boggy upland moors; all sorts of freshwater edges on migration.
When seen: All year round, but less common on shores in summer.
Breeds: Grassy nest on the ground, well hidden in grass or heather. 4 eggs.
Voice: A long shrill *dzee*, with nasal or grating quality, when put to flight.
Feeding: Takes insects, worms, etc. with a more continual action than the plovers.
Flight: Dashes and twists with large flocks which bank over and sweep down from a height, or swerve from side to side.

Pearly-grey above, white below

WINTER

White wing-bars on blackish background

WINTER

Black bill is short and straight

Black legs

Sanderlings chasing retreating waves on a sandy beach in winter

Marbled, rufous-brown above and on chest

White belly

Small, active, fast-moving wader, a fraction larger than *Dunlin*, with a straight bill. Never has black beneath.

Sanderling

SUMMER

Calidris alba   20cm/8″

Habitat: Flat, not rocky, shores with mud or sand.
When seen: Chiefly from August to May; often most numerous in spring.
Voice: A short. sharp, tuneless *twick*.
Feeding: More energetic than Dunlin. Picks for insects, worms, etc. on mud or sand.
Flight: Like Dunlin, but rarely in such large flocks, though often intermixed.

Pale stripe

Dull grey upper parts

Pale grey rump

Medium length bill

WINTER

Dull, whitish underparts

Greenish legs

Faint wing-stripe

Knot feeding in a dense mass on mud; they are very gregarious in winter

WINTER

Larger and dumpier than *Dunlin*. The lack of striking features, medium-length bill and short legs are useful clues.

Some birds retain summer plumage late in year

Richly variegated upper parts

Head and under-parts are orange-chestnut (see Dunlin, Bar-tailed Godwit)

Knot

SUMMER

Calidris canutus   25cm/10″

Habitat: Large estuaries, muddy shores.
When seen: Mostly from August to May; biggest numbers occur in winter.
Voice: A low *nut*; occasionally a liquid, whistling *quick-it*.
Feeding: Like Dunlin, but a little more sedate; often in much denser groups.
Flight: Like a heavy Dunlin; the largest flocks look like fast-moving smoke-clouds.

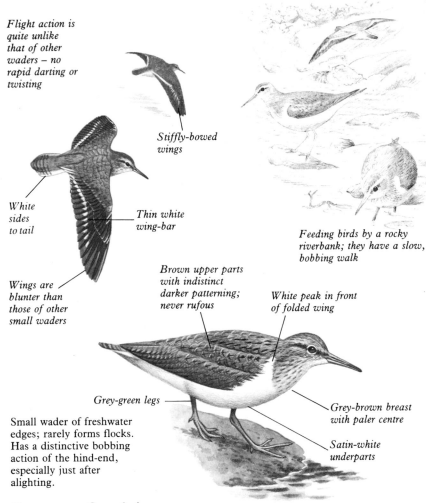

Flight action is quite unlike that of other waders – no rapid darting or twisting

Stiffly-bowed wings

White sides to tail

Thin white wing-bar

Feeding birds by a rocky riverbank; they have a slow, bobbing walk

Wings are blunter than those of other small waders

Brown upper parts with indistinct darker patterning; never rufous

White peak in front of folded wing

Grey-green legs

Small wader of freshwater edges; rarely forms flocks. Has a distinctive bobbing action of the hind-end, especially just after alighting.

Grey-brown breast with paler centre

Satin-white underparts

Common Sandpiper

Actitis hypoleucos   20cm/7¾"

Habitat: Less marine than most waders, but seen on all sorts of freshwater margins.
When seen: From April to October; a few in winter.
Breeds: Beside streams or upland lakes with shingly banks and boulders. 4 eggs.
Voice: A loud, ringing *twee-wee-weee*, tailing off; song is a variable rapid *kitti-deeit-kitti-deeit, kee-wee-dididid, tictictictic,* etc.
Feeding: Picks worms, molluscs, etc. from mud, stones and waterside vegetation.
Flight: Wings are held stiffly arched and flickered between momentary glides; usually flies very low but will go higher with more regular action.

Broad white band on trailing edge of wing

White rump

Brown upper parts (less grey than Greenshank, less well marked than Snipe)

Bill is red at base

Medium-sized wader with slender bill and long legs. White on rump and white band on wing are diagnostic.

Pale, speckled underparts

Vivid red legs

Redshanks in their breeding habitat

Redshank

Tringa totanus 28cm/11"
Habitat: Watermeadows, marshes, wet moorland; in winter, seashores, estuaries.
When seen: All year round.
Breeds: Nest is hidden in tall grass, often beneath a grassy canopy. 4 eggs.
Voice: Noisy, hysterical calls – high pitched *teuk, tuhu* and typically *teu-hu-hu*.
Feeding: Probes and picks worms, molluscs, etc. from mud, often in water.
Flight: Quicker than Ruff and more erratic than most large waders.

White rump and triangle on back (see Bar-tailed Godwit)

All-dark wings

Head and neck are often whiter than godwits'

Upper parts are greyer than Redshank's

Bill is slightly upcurved

Pale underparts

Similar shape to *Redshank* but with longer bill, longer neck and legs.

Grey-green legs

Greenshanks feed in water more often than Redshanks

Greenshank

Tringa nebularia 30cm/12"
Habitat: Estuaries, lakes, reservoirs in winter; wild, open moors and bogs in summer.
When seen: Chiefly on migration, but some breed in Scotland and some winter on coast.
Breeds: On the ground in open moorland or forest bogs. 4 eggs.
Voice: Loud, triple note, more even than Redshank's – *tew-tew-tew*.
Feeding and Flight: Like Redshank.

Faint white stripe

♀

Head projects as far forward as tail does behind

White sides to dark-centred rump

Female (all seasons) is like winter male, but 2-3" smaller.

Winter birds feeding on floodmeadows

Unmistakeable ruff and ear tufts, variable in colour

SUMMER ♂

Pinkish bill

Neatly scaled feathers with buff edges

Short bill, with no red

IMMATURE

Bright, buff-brown breast has faint streaks

Black feathers with white and buff edges

Buff-brown body

Head is often pale

WINTER ♂

Legs are red, orange, yellow, ochre, olive or green

Short, black, slightly curved bill

Variable medium-sized wader. Shortish, stout bill, round head on rather long neck, broad body tapering to pointed wing-tips and medium-long legs provide useful clues.

Ruff

Philomachus pugnax 22-30cm/8½-12" (male is larger)
Habitat: Wet grassy meadows in breeding season; otherwise marshes, reservoir edges, ploughed fields, floodmeadows.
When seen: Mostly in spring and autumn; breeds and winters in restricted areas.
Breeds: Males have communal displays at the 'hill' or 'lek', and females nest amongst grass and other vegetation near wet meadows. 4 eggs.
Voice: A quiet *tu-whit* is occasionally heard, but usually silent.
Feeding: Sedate feeding behaviour; picks and probes for worms, insects, etc. on ground.
Flight: Strong, steady wing-beats; a slower action than most waders.

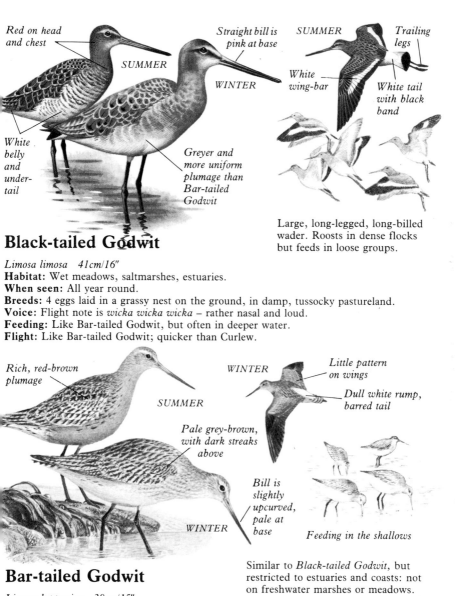

Red on head and chest

SUMMER

Straight bill is pink at base

WINTER

SUMMER

Trailing legs

White wing-bar

White tail with black band

White belly and under-tail

Greyer and more uniform plumage than Bar-tailed Godwit

Large, long-legged, long-billed wader. Roosts in dense flocks but feeds in loose groups.

Black-tailed Godwit

Limosa limosa 41cm/16"
Habitat: Wet meadows, saltmarshes, estuaries.
When seen: All year round.
Breeds: 4 eggs laid in a grassy nest on the ground, in damp, tussocky pastureland.
Voice: Flight note is *wicka wicka wicka* – rather nasal and loud.
Feeding: Like Bar-tailed Godwit, but often in deeper water.
Flight: Like Bar-tailed Godwit; quicker than Curlew.

Rich, red-brown plumage

SUMMER

WINTER

Little pattern on wings

Dull white rump, barred tail

Pale grey-brown, with dark streaks above

Bill is slightly upcurved, pale at base

WINTER

Feeding in the shallows

Similar to *Black-tailed Godwit*, but restricted to estuaries and coasts: not on freshwater marshes or meadows.

Bar-tailed Godwit

Limosa lapponica 38cm/15"
Habitat: Chiefly muddy seashores.
When seen: Mostly from August to March or April. Does not breed in W.Europe.
Voice: A low, nasal *kirric kirric*.
Feeding: Uses long bill to probe deeply in mud for crustaceans, molluscs, worms, etc.
Flight: Strong and quick, usually less erratic than Redshank.

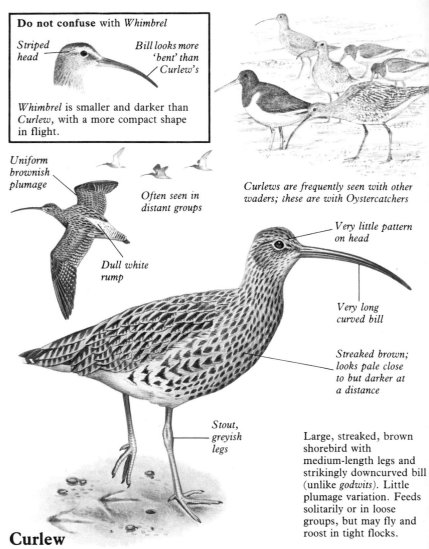

Do not confuse with *Whimbrel*

Striped head

Bill looks more 'bent' than Curlew's

Whimbrel is smaller and darker than *Curlew*, with a more compact shape in flight.

Uniform brownish plumage

Often seen in distant groups

Dull white rump

Curlews are frequently seen with other waders; these are with Oystercatchers

Very little pattern on head

Very long curved bill

Streaked brown; looks pale close to but darker at a distance

Stout, greyish legs

Large, streaked, brown shorebird with medium-length legs and strikingly downcurved bill (unlike *godwits*). Little plumage variation. Feeds solitarily or in loose groups, but may fly and roost in tight flocks.

Curlew

Numenius arquata 56cm/22"
Habitat: Moorland, wet meadows, arable land in summer; otherwise saltmarshes, muddy coasts, rocky shores.
When seen: All year round.
Breeds: Lays 4 large eggs in a scrape on the ground.
Voice: A loud *whaup, quoi quoi, cur-lee,* etc. with variations; loud, bubbling song.
Feeding: More sedate than most waders, probing for worms, crabs, etc.
Flight: Strong and quick but more gull-like than that of the smaller waders.

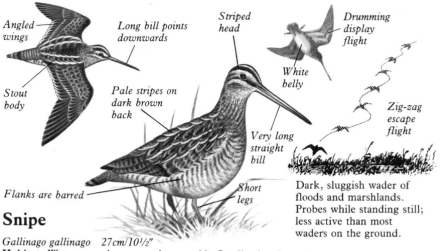

Angled wings

Long bill points downwards

Striped head

Drumming display flight

Stout body

White belly

Pale stripes on dark brown back

Zig-zag escape flight

Very long straight bill

Flanks are barred

Short legs

Dark, sluggish wader of floods and marshlands. Probes while standing still; less active than most waders on the ground.

Snipe

Gallinago gallinago   27cm/10½"

Habitat: Wet moors, bogs, marshes, muddy floodland, saltmarshes.
When seen: All year round.
Breeds: Lays 4 eggs, well hidden amongst grasses.
Voice: When flushed, a harsh *scaap*. In spring, a bright *chip-per chip-per chip-per*.
Produces a humming sound with outer tail feathers in diving display flight ('drumming').
Feeding: Probes in wet mud for worms etc. usually in dense cover.
Flight: When flushed, dashes off in erratic, twisting flight, gaining height quickly.

Rounded head is held up

Broader, less angled wings than Snipe

Crown is boldly barred (not striped)

Richly-marked brown upper-side

Long bill points down-wards

Long, straight bill

Roding flight at dusk

Woodcock

Secretive, cryptically-coloured woodland wader not seen on the shore.

Scolopax rusticola   34cm/13½"

Habitat: Mixed woodland with boggy spots, wet ditches.
When seen: All year round.
Breeds: Lays 4 eggs on woodland floor.
Voice: Flight note is a sharp whistle – *tsiwick;* also a deep croak in display.
Feeding: Like Snipe, but virtually always solitary, and usually at dusk.
Flight: Rapid escape flight; in display (called 'roding') wings are apparently beating slowly, but in fact have a rapid flickering motion.

Clear-cut black markings on white plumage (juvenile has brown smudges)

Long bluish legs

Slender, upcurved bill

Trailing legs

Slightly rounded wings

Avocets on a muddy estuary

Avocet

An unmistakeable, elegant, black and white wading bird. Can be 'lost' amongst flocks of *gulls*, but plumage pattern, long legs and upcurved bill are diagnostic.

Recurvirostra avosetta   43cm/17"
Habitat: Shallow, brackish water; muddy estuaries in winter in south-western Britain.
When seen: All year round.
Breeds: Lays 3 or 4 eggs in a scrape on dried mud. Most are on protected areas.
Voice: A loud, fluty whistle – *klute* or *kluit*.
Feeding: Sweeps bill sideways through shallow water for worms, molluscs, crustaceans.
Flight: Surprisingly quick flight action; rather short-winged shape.

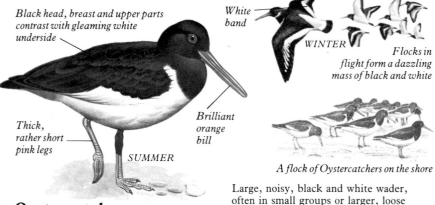

Black head, breast and upper parts contrast with gleaming white underside

White band

WINTER

Flocks in flight form a dazzling mass of black and white

Thick, rather short pink legs

Brilliant orange bill

SUMMER

A flock of Oystercatchers on the shore

Oystercatcher

Large, noisy, black and white wader, often in small groups or larger, loose aggregations.

Haematopus ostralegus   43cm/17"
Habitat: Sandy, muddy and rocky shores of an open nature; open grassy areas.
When seen: All year round.
Breeds: Lays 2-4 eggs in a scrape in shingle, sand or shell debris or in a hollow lined with pebbles etc. in short grass.
Voice: Noisy, high pitched *kleep kleep kleep, keeper keeper keeper, pik pik pik pik*.
Feeding: Keeps to the open, probing for cockles, opening mussels, etc.
Flight: Strong and quick; flocks fly in long lines, loose packs, etc.

Flash of white on outer primaries is distinctive

Grey under-wing, with white flash on outer primaries

SUMMER

Black-headed Gulls often feed inland

Wing pattern is distinctive, even on immature birds

WINTER

Scarlet bill with black tip

White head

WINTER

Brown patterning

IMMATURE

Dark red bill

Dark brown 'hood'

Black spot behind eye

WINTER

Swims with wing-tips angled upwards

Closed wing-tips are black with white streaks

A familiar, small gull. Active and agile; wings are often angled back, and are sharply pointed. Always shows flash of white on fore-edge of outer part of wing.

SUMMER

Pale grey wings

Dark red legs (scarlet in winter)

Black-headed Gull

Larus ridibundus   38cm/15"
Habitat: Breeds near upland pools, in wet pastures, dunes, saltmarshes, low islands; otherwise, almost anywhere.
When seen: All year round. Numbers increase in winter with influx from N. Europe.
Breeds: Variable nest often of reeds, rushes, grass, etc. near water. 2 or 3 eggs.
Voice: Varied raucous, screaming calls – *kwarr, kwup, kwee-ar*, etc.
Feeding: An opportunist; follows ploughs, searches fields, plunges into fresh or salt water, probes wet mud, etc. Takes fish, molluscs, insects, worms, berries, bread, etc.
Flight: Quick and fluid action but soars less than larger gulls; wing action is nearer that of terns; often performs twisting dives above feeding areas, etc.

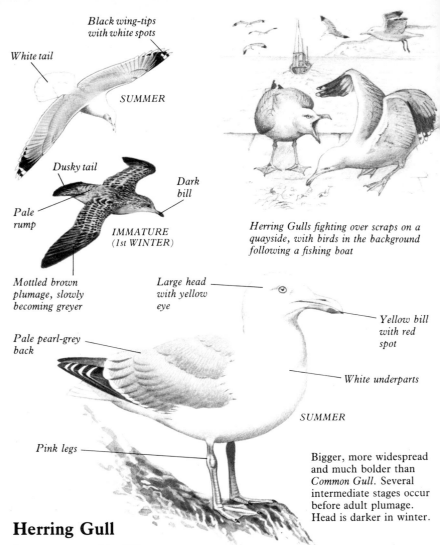

Black wing-tips
with white spots

White tail

SUMMER

Dusky tail

Dark
bill

Pale
rump

IMMATURE
(1st WINTER)

Herring Gulls fighting over scraps on a
quayside, with birds in the background
following a fishing boat

Mottled brown
plumage, slowly
becoming greyer

Large head
with yellow
eye

Yellow bill
with red
spot

Pale pearl-grey
back

White underparts

SUMMER

Pink legs

Bigger, more widespread
and much bolder than
Common Gull. Several
intermediate stages occur
before adult plumage.
Head is darker in winter.

Herring Gull

Larus argentatus   56cm/22"
Habitat: Breeds on cliffs, rocky islands, dunes; otherwise practically anywhere.
When seen: All year round, but seen inland mostly in winter, especially at rubbish tips.
Breeds: In a grass- or weed-lined scrape; often on roofs in seaside towns. 2 or 3 eggs.
Voice: Screaming seagull cries – *kyowww, kyow kyow kyow, kukukukuk, kyok,* etc.
Feeding: Active, opportunist, taking fish, crustaceans, etc. and all sorts of scraps and
carrion, fish from docks, offal from trawlers, rubbish, eggs and small birds.
Flight: Masterful – slipstreaming ships, soaring above cliffs. Direct flight is powerful
with shallow wing-beats. Flocks often fly in lines or in V-formation.

Smaller than *Herring Gull*, with a slightly darker back. Seen more often on playing fields, arable areas, etc.

Round head

Black wing-tips with white spots

Black band on white tail

IMMATURE

Striking white patch

Outer part of wing is all-dark

Pale greenish-yellow bill

Greenish legs

Common Gull

Common Gulls often feed inland

Larus canus 41cm/16"

Habitat: Moors near lakes, low offshore islands; in winter on muddy shores and inland.
When seen: All year round, but in the South, seen mostly in winter.
Breeds: In a grass-lined scrape in small colonies, amongst rocks, grass, heather, etc.
Voice: Higher pitched, more peevish than Herring Gull's.
Feeding: Takes worms, seeds, scraps, etc. Forages on grassland more than other gulls.
Flight: A little more fluent than Herring Gull, but soars less.

An oceanic gull, coming to cliffs to breed. Small and delicate, with slender, straight wings. Does not feed inland or on beaches.

Grey back and inner wing

WINTER

Black zig-zag

Black collar, spot and bill

IMMATURE

Small, greenish-yellow bill

Round white head with black eye

Darker back than Herring Gull

Black triangle (no white spots)

White tail is held low

SUMMER

Kittiwake

Kittiwakes nest on tiny cliff ledges

Rissa tridactyla 41cm/16"

Habitat: Open sea; sandy or rocky shores in summer; sheer cliffs. Rarely inland.
When seen: All year round but mostly at sea in winter.
Breeds: In colonies (often vast) on sheer cliffs; substantial nest. 2 or 3 eggs.
Voice: Noisy at colonies – loud, nasal *kitti-a-wak*, *kiarwark*, etc. Whining *whowww*.
Feeding: Takes fish etc. from surface of sea and some food from ground near colonies.
Flight: Superb soaring and gliding at breeding cliffs; swooping and gliding at sea.

Soaring and gliding

Head and bill like Herring Gull's

Grey wings blend into black tips

A large gull with a dark back about the same size as _Herring Gull_. Brown immatures are more like _Herring Gull_, but gradually develop dark grey colour above.

Yellow legs

IMMATURE

Primaries are all-dark

Lesser Black-backed Gull

Larus fuscus   53cm/21"
Habitat: Similar to Herring Gull, but breeds more frequently on dunes, islands, moors.
When seen: All year round.
Breeds: Lays 2-3 eggs in a grass-lined scrape on the ground, amongst vegetation.
Voice: Deeper, more throaty than Herring Gull's.
Feeding and Flight: Like Herring Gull; perhaps eats more eggs and young birds.

Head is larger than Herring Gull's

Long broad wings

Huge size makes it easy to identify

Gulls squabbling over scraps

Similar to _Lesser Black-backed_, but larger, with a darker back and pink legs. Immatures are more boldly chequered than immatures of _Herring Gull_.

Blackish back

Whitish or pale pink legs

Great Black-backed Gull

Larus marinus   66cm/26"
Habitat: Rocky coasts, islands, freshwater lakes near coast: estuaries in winter.
When seen: All year round.
Breeds: Often nests on prominent site on cliff-top or stack. 2-3 eggs.
Voice: Deeper than other gulls', less wailing – _owk, uh-uh-uh_, etc.
Feeding: More predatory than Herring Gull, taking more birds (including Puffins), mammals (such as rabbits) and carrion (such as dead sheep).
Flight: More ponderous than Herring Gull, but equally skilful.

Stiff-winged flight is unlike that of gulls

Wings may look blotchy with pale area on inner primaries, but no black tips

Grey tail and rump unlike any gull's

Large white head contrasts with grey upper parts

A colony of Fulmars on a sea cliff

Large, round, white head with black eye

Grey back

Stout, oddly-shaped bill (see gulls)

Dusky wing-tips

Even on cliff ledges, always sits, never stands

An ocean-going bird that is superficially *gull-like*. Flight, behaviour and (in close view) shape of head and bill are unlike gulls'. Never seen standing on quays, railings, etc. like a gull. Always sits, never stands.

Fulmar

Fulmarus glacialis   47cm/18½"
Habitat: The open sea; from mid-winter onwards, returns to coastal cliffs.
When seen: All year round, but mostly far out at sea in winter.
Breeds: On a ledge or in a cavity on coastal cliff or bank. One egg.
Voice: Loud choking or cackling noises at the nest.
Feeding: Takes fish, crustaceans, offal and other waste, often around ships.
Flight: Is masterly in wind or upcurrents above cliffs, gliding effortlessly with stiff wings; in calm weather, flight is low and heavier, with bursts of flapping.

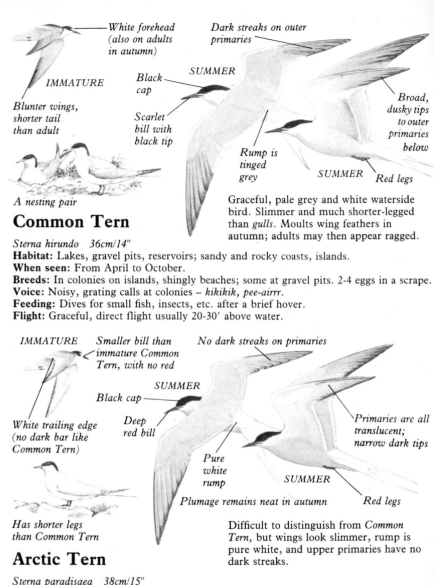

White forehead (also on adults in autumn)

Dark streaks on outer primaries

IMMATURE

SUMMER

Black cap

Broad, dusky tips to outer primaries below

Blunter wings, shorter tail than adult

Scarlet bill with black tip

Rump is tinged grey

SUMMER

Red legs

A nesting pair

Common Tern

Graceful, pale grey and white waterside bird. Slimmer and much shorter-legged than *gulls*. Moults wing feathers in autumn; adults may then appear ragged.

Sterna hirundo 36cm/14"

Habitat: Lakes, gravel pits, reservoirs; sandy and rocky coasts, islands.
When seen: From April to October.
Breeds: In colonies on islands, shingly beaches; some at gravel pits. 2-4 eggs in a scrape.
Voice: Noisy, grating calls at colonies – *kikikik, pee-airrr*.
Feeding: Dives for small fish, insects, etc. after a brief hover.
Flight: Graceful, direct flight usually 20-30' above water.

IMMATURE

Smaller bill than immature Common Tern, with no red

No dark streaks on primaries

SUMMER

Black cap

White trailing edge (no dark bar like Common Tern)

Deep red bill

Primaries are all translucent; narrow dark tips

Pure white rump

SUMMER

Plumage remains neat in autumn

Red legs

Has shorter legs than Common Tern

Arctic Tern

Difficult to distinguish from *Common Tern*, but wings look slimmer, rump is pure white, and upper primaries have no dark streaks.

Sterna paradisaea 38cm/15"

Habitat: Like Common Tern but more maritime and more frequent further north.
When seen: From April to October. Spring and autumn in the South.
Breeds: Often mixed with Common Tern but rarely inland. 1-3 eggs.
Voice: High, rising *keekee, pee-arr, kik kik*, etc.
Feeding: Like Common Tern.
Flight: Like Common Tern but, if anything, a little lighter. Head and neck look shorter.

Do not confuse with *Sandwich Tern*

Spiky crest   *Black bill with yellow tip*

Large coastal tern with black legs; gains white forehead by midsummer.

Little Terns plunge for food with a very fast dive after a flickering hover; they enter the water with a loud slap

Short, spiky tail

White forehead

Yellow bill

SUMMER

Pale grey above, with blackish outer primaries

Brownish markings

Darker bill than adult's

IMMATURE

WINTER

White forehead, even in spring (see other terns)

Yellow bill with black tip

SUMMER

Yellow legs

A tiny, fast-moving, energetic tern. Never has the full black cap of other terns. Essentially coastal. Yellow bill with black tip is diagnostic.

Little Tern

Sterna minuta   24cm/9½"

Habitat: Sand and shingle beaches, estuaries. Rarely inland.
When seen: From April to September.
Breeds: In small colonies on beaches. 2 or 3 eggs in a scrape close to the tideline.
Voice: Rapid chattering *kierri-kirri-kirri, kyik*, etc.
Feeding: Plunges for fish with a loud splash – a surprisingly violent dive for such a small bird. Like other terns, often seen carrying small fish in bill.
Flight: Less buoyant than other terns, with much quicker, flickering action; rapid wing-beats during hover.

Wings look straighter and broader when soaring

♂

Fans tail when soaring

Rufous upper parts

Long pointed wings

Kestrels often perch on wires, posts, etc. as well as hovering over open spaces looking for prey

Tail is closed in direct flight

♀

Dark wing-tips (♂ and ♀)

Typical appearance when hovering

Barred chestnut tail

Grey head

♂

♀

Rufous head

Typical pose of perched bird looking for prey on the ground

Red-brown back with large black spots

A common, small falcon, easily recognised by its slender shape and long wings and tail. Its most distinctive feature is its perfect hover. Female is slightly larger than male.

Long grey tail with black band

Kestrel

Falco tinnunculus   36cm/14"
Habitat: All types of open ground: moors, cliffs, farmland; also suburbs, towns.
When seen: All year round.
Breeds: Hollow trees, cliffs, old nests, buildings, even on the ground. 4-5 eggs.
Voice: A shrill, chattering *keekeekeekee.*
Feeding: Beetles, small rodents, worms, etc. May catch small birds.
Flight: Direct flight is regular and relatively slow; capable of swift chase or stoop. Hovers with head motionless; uses body and tail to compensate for wind changes.

♂

Black band
on tail

Dark brown
upper parts –
no rufous or
chestnut

♀ *Merlin flying fast and low over moorland*

More compact,
solid shape
than Kestrel

♀

Tail has
cream bars

Short wings
are broader-
based and taper
to a sharper
point than
Kestrel's

♀

Darker beneath
than Kestrel

Squarer head, more
alert expression
than Kestrel

♂

Blue-grey upper
parts – no brown

Orange-buff
underparts are
streaked with
brown

♂ is almost the
same size as a
Mistle Thrush;
♀ is larger

A small, dashing falcon of
wild, open country. Seen
less often than *Kestrel*, and
never on roadsides or in
suburban areas. More
compact than *Kestrel* and
never hovers.

Grey tail has
a black band

Merlin

Falco columbarius   Male 27cm/10½"; female 33cm/13"
Habitat: Heather moor, upland scrub, dunes, coastal marshes, etc.
When seen: All year round.
Breeds: On ground amongst heather or in the old nest of a crow. 4-5 eggs.
Voice: A shrill, rapid *wek-wek-wek-wek-wek*.
Feeding: Catches small birds in flight, after a rapid, twisting chase.
Flight: Faster, more dashing than Kestrel, often low down. Very agile; flies with rapid
wing-beats with very few glides. Rarely soars and never hovers.

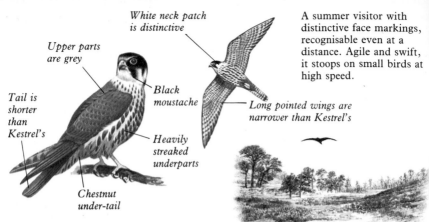

White neck patch is distinctive

Upper parts are grey

Tail is shorter than Kestrel's

Black moustache

Heavily streaked underparts

Chestnut under-tail

Long pointed wings are narrower than Kestrel's

A summer visitor with distinctive face markings, recognisable even at a distance. Agile and swift, it stoops on small birds at high speed.

Hobby soaring over heathland

Hobby

Falco subbuteo   36cm/14"
Habitat: Dry heaths, open woods, farmland with trees, marshes and lakes.
When seen: From April to October.
Breeds: Takes over a disused crow's nest in a pine or a deciduous tree. 2-4 eggs.
Voice: A high, whistling *kew kew kew kew.*
Feeding: Takes large insects such as bees or moths, also small birds.
Flight: Swift and manoeuvrable; quicker and more flexible than Kestrel. Rarely hovers.

Black moustache is broader than Hobby's

Grey upper parts

Long pointed wings

White chest and neck patch

Barred underparts

Large strong feet

Short broad tail and broad rump

A powerful bird with a heavy body, broad chest and strong feet. Capable of dramatic stoop in pursuit of prey.

Peregrine flying over sea cliffs

Peregrine

Falco peregrinus   38-48cm/15-19" (female is larger)
Habitat: Coasts, cliffs and mountainous country. Often over estuaries in winter.
When seen: All year round.
Breeds: On a cliff ledge, in a cavity or in an abandoned Raven's nest. 3-4 eggs.
Voice: Varied – a harsh rasping *kraah-kraah-kraah*, whining *keee-keee, keepk*, etc.
Feeding: Small- to medium-sized birds taken in the air after a chase or dive.
Flight: Masterly soaring; direct flight is rather pigeon-like, with quick regular beats.

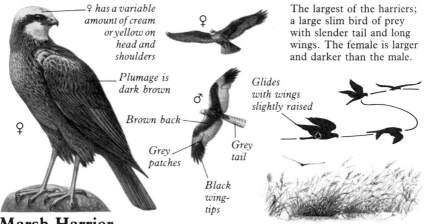

♀ has a variable amount of cream or yellow on head and shoulders

Plumage is dark brown

Brown back

Grey patches

Grey tail

Black wing-tips

Glides with wings slightly raised

The largest of the harriers; a large slim bird of prey with slender tail and long wings. The female is larger and darker than the male.

Marsh Harrier hunting just above a reedbed

Marsh Harrier

Circus aeruginosus 51-61cm/20-24" (female is usually larger)
Habitat: Large reed swamps or coastal meadows.
When seen: All year round.
Breeds: Builds its nest on the ground amongst reeds. 4-6 eggs.
Voice: Generally silent but has a chattering alarm call near the nest.
Feeding: Flies low over ground or marsh pouncing on small animals or birds.
Flight: Low except in display flight. Steady and slow; frequent glides on raised wings.

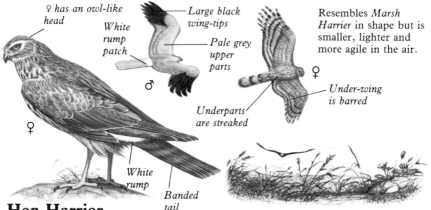

♀ has an owl-like head

White rump patch

Large black wing-tips

Pale grey upper parts

Resembles *Marsh Harrier* in shape but is smaller, lighter and more agile in the air.

Under-wing is barred

Underparts are streaked

White rump

Banded tail

Hen Harrier gliding with wings held in a shallow 'V'

Hen Harrier

Circus cyaneus 43-51cm/17-20" (female is larger)
Habitat: Moorland, extensive young plantations and estuaries.
When seen: All year round.
Breeds: Nests on the ground amongst heather or rushes in uplands. 4-6 eggs.
Voice: Male's call is a loud, rapid chatter – *chik-ik-ik-ik*; female's is less regular.
Feeding: As Marsh Harrier. Takes voles, mice, lizards, small birds, etc.
Flight: As Marsh Harrier but more agile. Buoyant, graceful action during glides.

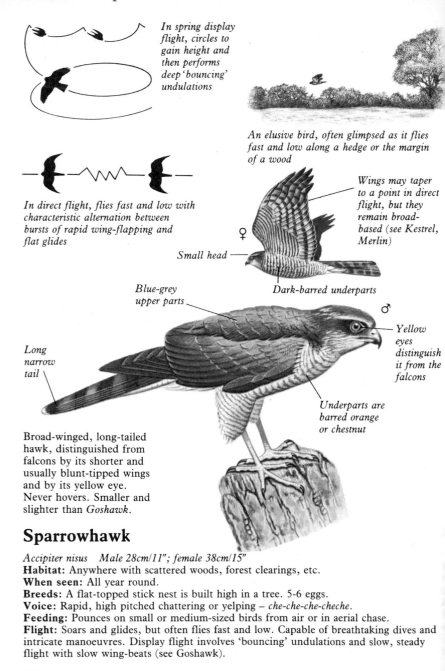

In spring display flight, circles to gain height and then performs deep 'bouncing' undulations

An elusive bird, often glimpsed as it flies fast and low along a hedge or the margin of a wood

In direct flight, flies fast and low with characteristic alternation between bursts of rapid wing-flapping and flat glides

Wings may taper to a point in direct flight, but they remain broad-based (see Kestrel, Merlin)

♀

Small head

Dark-barred underparts

Blue-grey upper parts

♂

Yellow eyes distinguish it from the falcons

Long narrow tail

Underparts are barred orange or chestnut

Broad-winged, long-tailed hawk, distinguished from falcons by its shorter and usually blunt-tipped wings and by its yellow eye. Never hovers. Smaller and slighter than *Goshawk*.

Sparrowhawk

Accipiter nisus   Male 28cm/11"; female 38cm/15"
Habitat: Anywhere with scattered woods, forest clearings, etc.
When seen: All year round.
Breeds: A flat-topped stick nest is built high in a tree. 5-6 eggs.
Voice: Rapid, high pitched chattering or yelping – *che-che-che-cheche*.
Feeding: Pounces on small or medium-sized birds from air or in aerial chase.
Flight: Soars and glides, but often flies fast and low. Capable of breathtaking dives and intricate manoeuvres. Display flight involves 'bouncing' undulations and slow, steady flight with slow wing-beats (see Goshawk).

Display flight is less acrobatic than Sparrowhawk's

Goshawks soar and display over their breeding territory in early spring, but otherwise fly below tree level and are very inconspicuous

IMMATURE

Underparts are buff with dark streaks

Large, fierce head

More massive than Sparrowhawk

♂

♀ is more the size of a Buzzard or broad-winged harrier

Head protrudes

♀

White under-tail

Deep broad chest

Rounded tip to broad tail

Barred under-parts

Male looks like a heavier version of the *Sparrowhawk* with a larger head, broader and longer wings. Female is huge and never suggests a *Sparrowhawk*. See *Buzzard, Peregrine*.

♀ resembles ♂ but is larger.

Goshawk

Accipiter gentilis   Male 48cm/19"; female 58cm/23"

Habitat: Well-wooded areas; forests with clearings or near moors, heaths, farmland.

When seen: All year round, but rare in Britain.

Breeds: Large nest of sticks is built in a large conifer or broadleaved tree. 3-4 eggs.

Voice: Screaming *hee-a* and chattering *gek-gek-gek*, reminiscent of Green Woodpecker.

Feeding: A powerful predator; takes prey in surprise dash from look-out perch or in aerial chase. Catches mammals such as squirrels, and birds such as pigeons, crows.

Flight: A series of flaps (less snappy than Sparrowhawk's), separated by long, direct glides (longer than Sparrowhawk's). The wings are curved back to a point during glides.

Short, broad tail is fanned when soaring

Long wings are broad and rounded when soaring

Short, broad head

Darker carpal patch

Brown plumage with blotches and bars (see immature Golden Eagle)

Pale area on flight feathers

Black wing-tips

Glides with tail closed

Stout, hooked bill

Rounded head

Glides on flexed wings

Several Buzzards may be seen soaring in wide circles together

Soars for long periods, circling in wide spirals without flapping; wing-tips are upcurved and wings are held in a shallow 'V'

Brown, cream and black plumage is very variable – may be pale with large areas of cream

Perched bird looks upright and solid

Our commonest large bird of prey, often seen on roadside poles or trees, on the ground in fields or soaring in circles over woods, farmland or moors. More heavily built than the *harriers*.

Buzzard

Buteo buteo   51-56cm/20-22" (female is usually larger)
Habitat: Well-wooded districts adjacent to lowland heath or upland moor; pasture with hedges and copses, especially in broad valleys; open coastal areas.
When seen: All year round.
Breeds: Builds a bulky stick nest in the fork of a tree or on a cliff. 2-4 eggs.
Voice: Loud, far-carrying and powerful *pee-ah* and other more plaintive variants.
Feeding: Live prey, especially rabbits; also voles, small birds, beetles, worms, etc.
Flight: Rather heavy with short glides and stiffish wing-beats. Also hovers and soars.

IMMATURE – same huge size as adult, but with blacker plumage

Large white
wing patches

Black band
on white tail

Closes tail
when gliding

Golden Eagle soaring along a mountainside, with wings slightly raised

Brown
plumage
can look
nearly black
in flight

Wings are long
and broad
with fingered
wing-tips

'Switchback' display flight: deep, undulating swoops with wing-tips folded into tail and 'shoulders' out

Head and
bill
protrude

Bulging trailing edge

Fans broad tail when
soaring – longer than
Buzzard's

Large head and bill

Massive
'shoulders'

Huge, dark bird of prey
found in wild moorland,
remote cliffs and
mountains. Unlike
Buzzard, does not frequent
roadsides or farmland and
is rarely seen close to.

Heavily feathered
legs and
powerful feet

Golden Eagle

Aquila chrysaetos 76-89cm/30-35" (female is usually larger)
Habitat: Chiefly wild mountainous areas; also forests and coastal cliffs.
When seen: All year round.
Breeds: Often reuses the same huge nest on a cliff ledge or in a tree. 2 eggs.
Voice: Generally silent, but a whistling note or shrill *kea* may be heard.
Feeding: Eats carrion; also hunts rabbits, hares, grouse, crows, etc.
Flight: Direct flight is powerful and impressive with deep, regular wing-flaps and long glides. Soars magnificently, looking more steady than *Buzzard*. Capable of great speed.

Typical hovering pose before diving into water to catch fish

Black carpal patches are characteristic

Osprey plunging into water with a great splash to catch fish; it does not usually submerge completely

Translucent, barred tail

Head is whitish with a broad black band

Crested head

Rich brown upper parts (juvenile's are barred buff)

Wings are very long and often slightly angled at the carpal joint

Brownish band across white underparts

A fish-eating raptor bigger than a *Buzzard*. At a distance its wing-shape (a shallow, inverted 'W') may suggest a large gull.

Stout blue legs

Osprey

Pandion haliaetus   51-58cm/20-23"
Habitat: Large lakes, reservoirs, rivers and sheltered coasts.
When seen: From April to October.
Breeds: Builds a huge stick nest in a tree, often near water. 3 eggs.
Voice: High pitched, rapid, emphatic whistle: *chew chew chew chew chew.*
Feeding: Almost exclusively fish: hovers then plunge-dives feet first from the air.
Flight: Direct flight is steady with regular wing-beats; also soars, hovers and circles over water when looking for fish. Wings are flexible and powerful.

Dark-breasted Barn Owl
is found in parts of Europe

Orange-buff or golden-brown
with a fine freckling of grey
and white

White
'monkey'
face with
black
eyes

White
underparts

Long, slim
white legs

Barn Owl in the moonlight,
looking pale and ghostly

Barn Owl

A common owl of farmland
with a distinctive white
'monkey' face. Mostly
nocturnal. Often seen in car
headlight beams.

Tyto alba   36cm/14"
Habitat: Mixed farmland, open country, bogs and marshes.
When seen: All year round.
Breeds: Barns, church towers, holes in trees, etc. Often 2 broods. 4-7 eggs.
Voice: Hissing and snoring notes; *kit-ik;* a long shriek.
Feeding: Drops on to small rodents, birds, beetles, etc. from low hunting flight.
Flight: Low and wavering, graceful and agile: turns sharply to drop on prey.

Flattened
head

Yellow
eyes

Upper parts
are dark
brown with
pale spots

Streaked
underparts

Undulating flight in
open country, fields, etc.

The Little Owl is often seen in
daylight, but hunts at dusk

Little Owl

A small, dark owl with a
fierce expression. It bobs
its head and stretches its
neck when alert.

Athene noctua   22cm/8½"
Habitat: Mixed farmland with trees; farmsteads; coastal cliffs, etc.
When seen: All year round.
Breeds: In hollow trees, farm buildings, cavities in rocks, etc. 3-5 eggs.
Voice: Pleasing, high-pitched *kiew, kleeee-ok,* etc.
Feeding: Catches beetles, worms, rodents and some small birds.
Flight: Less aerial than larger owls. Undulating flight is almost woodpecker-like.

Tawny Owl returning to its nest with its prey – a vole

Tawny Owls may be discovered at their daytime roosts by following up noisy mobbing by small birds

Very short tail

Bulky head and body

Enormous round head

Broad, rounded wings

Pale spots on wing coverts

Black eyes

Brown plumage is streaked and mottled

A common large owl of woodlands, parks and wooded gardens. It hunts by night and is the owl which emits the eerie and familiar hoot.

Tawny Owl

Strix aluco   38cm/15"
Habitat: Woodland, parkland and wooded suburbia.
When seen: All year round.
Breeds: In hollow tree, sometimes old crow's nest; uses no nesting material. 2-4 eggs.
Voice: Varied *kewick, kvick,* etc.; classic hoot, *hoo-oo-oo-hoooooooooooooo.*
Feeding: Nocturnal; takes voles, mice, rats, small birds, frogs, worms, etc.
Flight: Fairly rapid and direct; heavier than other owls. Less aerial than Barn or 'eared' owls, drops on to prey from a perch rather than from the air.

Birds flying low over marshland; they quarter the ground like harriers

Short ear-tufts

Dark patch

Dark patch

Pale wing patch

Large, rounded head with vivid yellow eyes

Streaked breast and silky-white underparts (see Long-eared Owl)

A large, rather fierce-looking owl which hunts at dusk or in the daytime and prefers open country. Perches on the ground.

Upper parts are mottled and streaked (less red than Tawny)

Short-eared Owl

Asio flammeus   38cm/15"
Habitat: Bogs, marshes, moorland, grassland, sometimes clearings in open woodland.
When seen: All year round, but mostly in lowland areas during winter.
Breeds: On the ground amongst heather, rushes, etc. 4-7 eggs.
Voice: Deep, barking *boo-boo-boo* in display flight; squawking *kwowk*.
Feeding: Hunts in daylight or at dusk, taking voles and other small mammals.
Flight: Low and wavering, but sometimes very high. Hovers briefly.

Strongly marked face pattern and orange eyes

Long ear-tufts may be visible

Dark patch

Long-eared Owls roost in the day, often in conifers

Underside is streaked – no white

Pale wing patch

A secretive, night-hunting owl of dense coniferous woods. Long 'ears' are not visible in flight.

Wings are closely barred

Plumage may be yellower or greyer than Tawny's

Long-eared Owl

Asio otus   34cm/13½"
Habitat: Edges of dense woodland, copses, willow thickets, etc.
When seen: All year round.
Breeds: In an old crow's nest, etc. 3-6 eggs.
Voice: Deep, groaning hoot; young give high pitched *kee-kiew* like a squeaky hinge.
Feeding: Nocturnal; takes rodents and small birds.
Flight: Like Short-eared Owl.

Glides on arched wings

♂

Slender neck is extended in flight

Distinctive black and white markings on under-wing

A common gamebird of moorland. Usually creeps through the heather with its body close to the ground but sometimes stands erect with body held higher and neck and head upright.

Red wattle over eye

Red Grouse standing sentinel-like; in the background, a flock rises with a whirring sound.

♂

Larger, darker and redder than Partridge

Obvious blackish-brown tail

Plumage is browner and more speckled than on ♂

♀

Red Grouse

Lagopus lagopus scoticus 38cm/15″
Habitat: Open moorland, principally heather.
When seen: All year round.
Breeds: Lays 6-11 eggs well hidden in heather or long grass.
Voice: Outbursts of cackling notes – *kowk; kowk-kok-ok-ok-ok; b'k b'k k'k-k-k-k-k; bak-gobak-gobak-bakakakak*, etc.
Feeding: Young heather shoots, buds and berries from low-growing plants, etc.
Flight: Rapid escape flight is low and direct with bursts of rapid wing-beats between glides on arched wings. Faster than Partridge; looks bigger and long-necked.

Orange face patch

Brown upper parts are streaked with cream

Chestnut tail

Broad, downcurved wings

Grey breast

A dumpy, rounded slightly chicken-like bird with a small head, short legs and tail but a bulky body. Orange patch on face is diagnostic.

Brown 'horseshoe' on ♂

Partridges are often seen in groups on farmland in winter

Grey Partridge

Perdix perdix   30cm/12"
Habitat: Mixed agricultural land, heaths, dunes and waste areas.
When seen: All year round.
Breeds: Lays eggs in a scrape amongst crops, under bushes, etc. 9-20 eggs.
Voice: *Kit-it-it* when flushed; grating, creaky *kierr-ic.*
Feeding: Young shoots, seeds, grain, insects, etc. picked from the ground.
Flight: Whirring wing-beats between glides on downcurved wings.

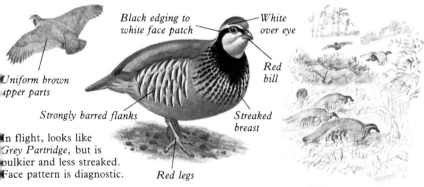

Black edging to white face patch

White over eye

Red bill

Uniform brown upper parts

Strongly barred flanks

Streaked breast

In flight, looks like Grey Partridge, but is bulkier and less streaked. Face pattern is diagnostic.

Red legs

Birds scurrying for cover and skimming a hedge – they are reluctant to fly

Red-legged Partridge

Alectoris rufa   34cm/13½"
Habitat: Farmland, sandy heaths and commons, dunes.
When seen: All year round.
Breeds: Lays eggs in a well concealed nest on the ground. 10-16 eggs.
Voice: *Kuk-kuk* when flushed; *chuk-ar chuka-chuka* and 'steam engine' noises.
Feeding: Vegetable matter, slugs, beetles, etc. taken from the ground.
Flight: Flies less than Grey Partridge but looks similar in the air.

♂

Typical view of Pheasant flying away

Short, broad, downcurved wings

♂

♂ often has a white neck-ring

Pointed tail

♀

Pheasants feeding on stubble in winter

Ear tufts

Red wattle on dark head

♂

Colourful, glossy plumage

Crescent markings on breast and flanks

Long, pointed tail

A common gamebird unmistakeable when full-grown but part-grown juveniles may be confused with *Partridge*. Small head, bulky body and pointed tail are distinctive on adults.

♀

Dull, mottled brown plumage

Pheasant

Phasianus colchicus   Female 53cm/21"; male 89cm/35"
Habitat: Parkland, woodland edges, plantations and reedbeds.
When seen: All year round.
Breeds: Nest is well hidden on the ground. 8-15 eggs.
Voice: A crowing *korr-kok* together with drumming of wings.
Feeding: Walks sedately along the edges of fields or through thick cover taking insects, worms, seeds, berries, shoots, etc.
Flight: When disturbed, bursts suddenly from cover, with rapid, noisy wing-beats. Direct flight is fast with long glides. Juveniles can fly when quite small.

Claps
wings

Glides

In undulating display flight, the bird stalls at the top of each steep climb, claps its wings over its body and glides

Woodpigeons feeding on a stubble field in summer; they often feed in very large flocks

Pale
rump

White wing patches
at all ages

Dark
tail

Powerful
wings

Brownish
back

Small, round
head

White neck patch
on adults (not
on juveniles)

Pink breast

Deep, rounded
chest

Greyish
rump

Greyish
wings

The largest member of the pigeon family, the Woodpigeon is distinguished by its small head and relatively stout body, long neck, wings and tail. Common in arable areas, but also seen in towns.

Woodpigeon

Columba palumbus   41cm/16"
Habitat: Mixed woodland, open fields, parks and suburbia.
When seen: All year round.
Breeds: Stick nest, often thin and flimsy at almost any height in tree or bush. 2 eggs.
Voice: Typical soft, pleasant cooing – *cu-cooo-coo, coo-coo.* No flight call.
Feeding: Grain and other vegetable matter chiefly taken from the ground, also buds and berries of trees, ivy, etc.
Flight: Strong, fast flight with rapid, deep wing-beats. Escape flight is swift and steep with clattering wings. Large flocks may be strung out over long distances.

Two dark bars on inner wing

No white on wings – instead, has a pale central area bordered with dark grey and black (see Woodpigeon)

Smoky-grey under-wing (see Feral Pigeon)

Stock Doves feed in fields, usually in small flocks and often with Woodpigeons

In flight, shows narrow wings, slender tail and short, round head

No white patch on neck (see Woodpigeon)

Blue-grey back with no brown

Pink breast

A fairly common pigeon, smaller, darker and bluer than *Woodpigeon*.

Stock Dove

Columba oenas   33cm/13"
Habitat: Woods, parks, farmland with old trees, cliffs and rocky coasts.
When seen: All year round.
Breeds: No real nest; lays eggs in hollow tree, cavity in building or cliff. 2 eggs.
Voice: Deep rhythmic *ooo-woo* with emphasis on the second syllable.
Feeding: Grain and all sorts of vegetable matter from the ground. Feeds in flocks.
Flight: Strong with deep, rapid wing-beats, like Woodpigeon but faster. Gliding display flight. Looks broader-winged, rounder-headed than Feral Pigeon.

Do not confuse with *Rock Dove*

Pale grey back

Square, white rump patch

Dark head and neck

Two dark bars on wings

Found on coastal cliffs and adjacent farmland, rocky islands, etc.

Feral Pigeons are a common sight in cities; they land and take off with a lot of clatter

Often has white patches on wings – or white wings

Under-wing is sometimes white

Fleshy area at base of bill is larger than on other pigeons

Tail is widely fanned for landing

Feral Pigeons are domestic pigeons that have gone wild. They are descended from the truly wild *Rock Dove*, from which they are sometimes almost indistinguishable.

Plumage is very variable – can be blue, grey, brown, white or chequered

Feral Pigeon

Columba livia   33cm/13"
Habitat: Almost anywhere around towns, railway yards or farmland.
When seen: All year round.
Breeds: Builds nest, which may be substantial, on a ledge in a cave or building. 2 eggs.
Voice: Familiar rolling, purring *coo.*
Feeding: Chiefly vegetable matter; in towns, takes all sort of scraps. Feeds on the ground with familiar waddling walk, picking up food as it goes.
Flight: Swift and direct; capable of rapid, swooping dives. Protruding head.

73

Streaked patch on side of neck

Black tail with white 'V'-shaped tip both above and below

Chestnut back with dark spots

A pair of Turtle Doves – a familiar sight in summer

Grey patch on wings

Turtle Dove

A small, delicate dove of woods and farmland – slimmer than *Collared Dove*.

Streptopelia turtur   28cm/11"
Habitat: Woodlands, parks and tall hedges.
When seen: From April to August.
Breeds: A flimsy, thin nest is built in a tree or hedge. 2 eggs.
Voice: Purring *rroorrr- rrrr- rroorrooorrrr* – a pleasant summertime sound.
Feeding: Green plants (fumitory, etc.), seeds.
Flight: Lighter and quicker than Collared Dove with swept-back wings.

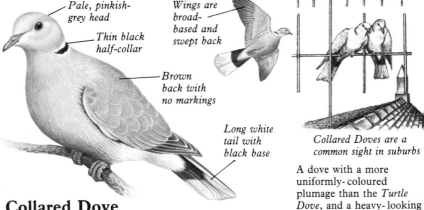

Pale, pinkish-grey head

Wings are broad-based and swept back

Thin black half-collar

Brown back with no markings

Long white tail with black base

Collared Doves are a common sight in suburbs

Collared Dove

A dove with a more uniformly- coloured plumage than the *Turtle Dove*, and a heavy- looking action in flight.

Streptopelia decaocto   28cm/11"
Habitat: Well wooded parks and suburbs, docks, distilleries, etc.
When seen: All year round.
Breeds: Builds a frail nest in dense evergreen or a thick hedge. 2 eggs.
Voice: Monotonous, abrupt *cu-cooo-cuk* and a throaty, nasal *kwurrr*.
Feeding: Eats grain and other seeds, scraps, berries, etc.
Flight: Direct but less swift than other pigeons; deep, rather floppy wing-beats.

JUVENILE

♀ *is sometimes a similar colour to juvenile, but ♀ and ♂ are usually grey*

The Cuckoo is usually glimpsed only fleetingly as it flies across clearings in woods or heaths

Head is held high

Tail is half-fanned in flight

Wings are swept back and are flapped below body level

Small grey head and grey throat

Grey back

Tail is speckled with white

An elusive bird, often the *cooc-coo* call is the only clue to its presence.

Dark grey bars on chest

Cuckoo

Cuculus canorus   33cm/13″

Habitat: Moorland, heaths, marshes and farmland.
When seen: From April to September.
Breeds: Lays up to 12 eggs, each in a separate nest of a host species such as Dunnock, Robin, Pied Wagtail, Meadow Pipit, Reed Warbler.
Voice: Familiar *cooc-coo;* female has a liquid, throaty, bubbling call. Also a harsh, laughing *hek-ek-ek*.
Feeding: Insects, especially caterpillars, taken from the ground.
Flight: Low and quick with fast wing-beats, swooping up to a perch. Usually more jerky than Kestrel, more continual flapping than Sparrowhawk.

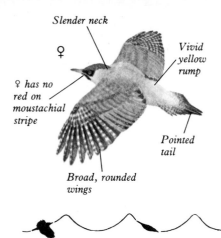

Slender neck

♀

♀ has no red on moustachial stripe

Vivid yellow rump

Pointed tail

Broad, rounded wings

Undulating flight: bursts of rapid wing-beats alternate with swoops on closed wings

Green Woodpeckers are often seen away from trees on open ground, especially near anthills, from which they feed

Red crown

Black patch around white eye

♂ has a red patch on moustachial stripe

Stout grey bill

♂

Neck and underparts are pale greenish-grey (closely barred on juveniles)

Soft green upper parts

A large woodpecker of deciduous woods, scrubby heaths and open ground. Our only large green bird; the vivid yellow rump is distinctive.

Green Woodpecker

Picus viridis   32cm/12½"

Habitat: Deciduous woodland, parks, heaths, coastal areas and sand dunes.
When seen: All year round.
Breeds: Excavates a round hole in a tree. 5-7 eggs.
Voice: Loud, ringing notes – *kew kew kew kew* and *kyow-yow-yow-yow* with variations.
Feeding: Takes all kinds of small insect food from trees and from open ground.
Flight: Quick and deeply undulating.

Pale pointed bill

Head is held well back before striking – a useful identification point even at a distance

♂

♂ has red crown

Slender neck

♀ has red patch on nape

♀

Long, broad wings

Pointed tail

Plumage is all-black apart from head

Long tail

A huge, powerful woodpecker, **not found in Britain,** but found in many other parts of Europe. In posture and behaviour, it resembles other woodpeckers.

Black Woodpecker

Dryocopus martius   46cm/18"
Habitat: Mature beechwoods and large coniferous forests.
When seen: All year round; never in Britain.
Breeds: A large nest hole is excavated in a tree trunk. 4-6 eggs.
Voice: A ringing *chock-chock-chock.*
Feeding: Eats insects, especially ants.
Flight: Quick, strong but undulating.

Great Spotted Woodpecker looking for insects

A richly coloured, glossy, very handsome bird, smaller than *Green Woodpecker*. Climbs vertical trunks using its stiff tail as a support.

Great Spotted Woodpecker

Dendrocopos major   23cm/9"
Habitat: All kinds of woodland, scrub.
When seen: All year round.
Breeds: Makes an oval nest-hole in a tree. 4-7 eggs.
Voice: Loud, sharp *tchick*; rattling *tchikikeekee*. Short, loud drumming with bill.
Feeding: Takes insects, nuts, seeds, berries, etc. from trees.
Flight: Steeply undulating flight typical of all woodpeckers.

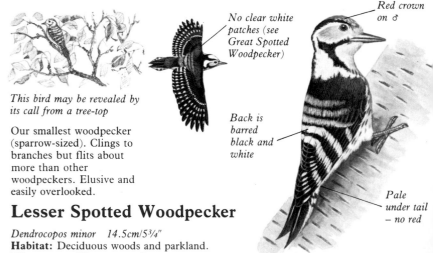

This bird may be revealed by its call from a tree-top

Our smallest woodpecker (sparrow-sized). Clings to branches but flits about more than other woodpeckers. Elusive and easily overlooked.

Lesser Spotted Woodpecker

Dendrocopos minor   14.5cm/5¾"
Habitat: Deciduous woods and parkland.
When seen: All year round.
Breeds: Excavates a small hole in soft wood. 4-6 eggs.
Voice: Loud, nasal *pee-pee-pee-pee-pee-pee*. Weaker drumming than Great Spotted.
Feeding: Feeds amongst thin, high twigs more often than other woodpeckers.
Flight: Like other woodpeckers, but weaker and more fluttering.

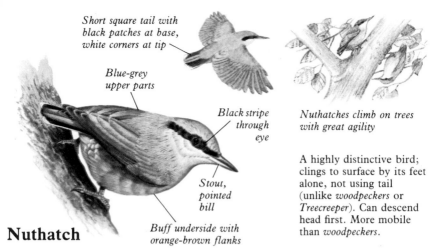

Short square tail with black patches at base, white corners at tip

Blue-grey upper parts

Black stripe through eye

Stout, pointed bill

Buff underside with orange-brown flanks

Nuthatches climb on trees with great agility

Nuthatch

A highly distinctive bird; clings to surface by its feet alone, not using tail (unlike *woodpeckers* or *Treecreeper*). Can descend head first. More mobile than *woodpeckers*.

Sitta europaea   14cm/5½"
Habitat: Deciduous woods; trees in parks and gardens.
When seen: All year round.
Breeds: In a hole in a tree; plasters the entrance with mud to reduce size. 6-9 eggs.
Voice: Varied: ringing *witwitwitwitwit*; loud, rapid trill; fluty whistles, etc.
Feeding: Takes nuts, berries, seeds, insects, etc. from trees or ground beneath.
Flight: Quick, flitting action over short distances.

Upperside is brown with pale mottles

Slender, down-curved bill

Dark and pale bars on wing

Silvery white underside is often dingy on flanks

Treecreepers climb trees using their tail as a support

Treecreeper

An unobtrusive brown bird which creeps up tree trunks and along branches. It can also hang under branches using its feet alone. Song and call are useful when trying to locate it.

Certhia familiaris   12.5cm/5"
Habitat: Woodland of all kinds, parks.
When seen: All year round.
Breeds: Builds nest behind loose bark, etc. 5-6 eggs.
Voice: Bright, thin song ends in a flourish; call is a thin, high *tseee*.
Feeding: Spirals or creeps up tree trunks with jerky hops; takes small insects, spiders.
Flight: Weak, but less undulating than that of Nuthatch.

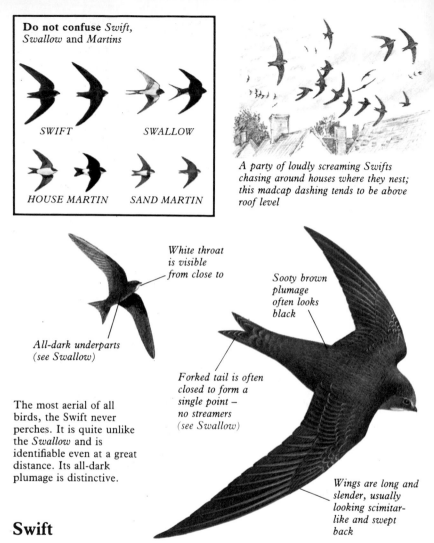

Do not confuse *Swift,*
Swallow and *Martins*

SWIFT   SWALLOW

HOUSE MARTIN   SAND MARTIN

A party of loudly screaming Swifts
chasing around houses where they nest;
this madcap dashing tends to be above
roof level

White throat
is visible
from close to

Sooty brown
plumage
often looks
black

All-dark underparts
(see Swallow)

Forked tail is often
closed to form a
single point –
no streamers
(see Swallow)

The most aerial of all
birds, the Swift never
perches. It is quite unlike
the *Swallow* and is
identifiable even at a great
distance. Its all-dark
plumage is distinctive.

Wings are long and
slender, usually
looking scimitar-
like and swept
back

Swift

Apus apus   16.5cm/6½"
Habitat: The open air above any kind of terrain – especially over houses, lakes, marshes.
When seen: From the end of April to August or September.
Breeds: Loosely colonial; nests in cavities in buildings, under eaves, etc. A few still
nest in natural holes in cliffs. 2-3 eggs.
Voice: Loud screeching, especially from chasing parties around breeding sites.
Feeding: Takes insects only in the air, concentrating over water in bad weather.
Flight: Fast; rapid, stiff, flickering wing-beats between glides. In fine weather is usually
high in the air, but on muggy or wet days is low down over water or fields.

Pale underparts (not brilliant white like House Martin's)

White on tail shows when tail is fanned

Swallows flying around a farmyard; they tend to swoop up into barns from low levels, to visit their nests

Glossy blue plumage may look black

Forked tail has long streamers (shorter ones on juvenile)

Red patch over bill and on throat

No white on rump (see House Martin)

The most graceful and supple of all the swallows and martins. Often seen perching on roofs, wires or bare twigs. Less common in suburban areas than *House Martin*. Red on throat, forked tail and long streamers are diagnostic.

Wings are broader and more supple than Swift's

Swallow

Hirundo rustica 19cm/7½"

Habitat: Open areas close to suitable breeding sites; lakes, reservoirs, reedbeds, etc.
When seen: From April to September or October.
Breeds: Makes a nest of mud and grasses supported by a rafter in a barn, shed, or other building. 2 broods. 4-6 eggs.
Voice: A pleasant, twittering *tswit-wit-wit* and a warbling song with short trills.
Feeding: Catches insects in flight, often over meadows or water, usually low down.
Flight: Easy, swerving, skimming flight at low level; less fluttering than the martins and less dashing than the Swift.

Characteristic mud nest is built beneath the eaves of houses, under bridges and in similar situations

House Martins swoop and glide at or above roof level – usually higher than Swallows

Wings are stiffer than Swallow's and are held flat during glides

Brilliant all-white underparts

Fanned tail looks triangular

Glossy blue back often looks black

Small bill

White chin

Forked tail, but no long streamers (see Swallow)

Wings look browner than the back

Broad white patch on rump

A small bird which feeds in the air during its fluttery flight. The broad white patch on the rump is diagnostic.

House Martin

Delichon urbica   12.5cm/5"
Habitat: Near dwellings of all kinds: suburban areas, villages, farmyards, etc.
When seen: From April to October.
Breeds: Collects mud from ground for nest. 2 or 3 broods. 4-5 eggs.
Voice: *Chirrup.* Twittering song is less warbling than Swallow's.
Feeding: An aerial feeder but often at higher levels than Swallow.
Flight: Less supple in the air than Swallow, swoops more stiffly and has more fluttering wing-beats. Slower and less dashing than Swift.

Flutters up to nest hole in a vertical sand-bank

A group of Sand Martins at their nest holes in a steep bank of sand; they favour sites near water

Upper parts are sandy-brown with no white or blue (see House Martin)

White underparts may be slightly soiled with sand – so are less brilliantly white than House Martin's

White throat

Brown breast-band

The smallest of the swallows and martins, with the most fluttery flight. Feeds in the air but flocks sometimes gather on level ground. Often seen over water.

Sand Martin

Riparia riparia 12cm/4¾"

Habitat: Sand-banks near rivers, lakes and gravel pits.
When seen: April to September, although some may be seen in March.
Breeds: Excavates nest holes in steep banks of sand. 2 broods. 4-5 eggs.
Voice: A dry *chirp* which develops into a twittering song.
Feeding: Takes insects in flight, often low over water or reeds.
Flight: Similar to House Martin but weaker and more fluttering; more erratic and less graceful than Swallow but nevertheless an expert in the air.

Hovers and sings

In song flight, rises vertically into the air, hovers at a considerable height and then plummets towards the ground, singing all the time

Skylarks often form large flocks in winter

Short head

Broad wings taper almost to a point

Pale trailing edge of wing

White sides to tail

Stocky body

Speckled crest may be raised or flat

Short, stout bill

Also sings from a perch

Very long hind claw

Streaked gorget contrasts with silvery-white underparts

Upper parts are sandy with dark and light streaks

Small, stocky bird of open spaces, with speckled crest and heavily streaked plumage. It is smaller than the *thrushes* and heavier than the *pipits*. Famous for its remarkable and beautiful song.

Skylark

Alauda arvensis   18cm/7"
Habitat: Open farmland, golf links, dunes, moorland and saltmarsh.
When seen: All year round.
Breeds: Nest is well concealed on the ground. 2 broods. 3-5 eggs.
Voice: Rippling, liquid *chirrup*, high thin *tswee* from flocks in flight. Song may be of several minutes' duration: liquid, warbling and harsh notes blended together.
Feeding: Takes seeds, insects, worms, etc. from open ground.
Flight: Slightly jerky and undulating when flushed; over long distances, there are short pauses between bursts of wing-beats.

Orange-buff sides to tail – no white (see Skylark)

Plumage is often paler than Skylark's

Long pointed crest

No pale trailing edge on wing

Pinkish-orange under-wing

Looks very like a *Skylark*, but is paler, has broader wings and shorter tail. Crest is more conspicuous. **Hardly ever seen in Britain.**

Breast is strongly marked

Crested Lark

Galerida cristata   16.5cm/6½"

Crested Lark singing with crest fully raised

Habitat: Open fields, dunes and sandy areas.

When seen: All year round, but normally not found in Britain.

Breeds: Nest is well concealed on the ground. 3-5 eggs.

Voice: Fluty whistles – *doo-dl-ee, whee-dl-eedloo,* etc. louder, clearer than Skylark. Song includes similar notes to Skylark's, but is less flowing.

Feeding: Like the Skylark.

Flight: Floppier, more undulating flight than Skylark's.

Black and white patch

Circling song flight

Pointed crest

Fine bill

Broad pale stripe over eye

Short tail has black and white corners

Breast is finely streaked

Smaller than other larks but with broad wings which make it look larger in flight.

Woodlark singing from a perch

Woodlark

White on corners of tail only

Lullula arborea   15cm/6"

Habitat: Sandy heaths, the edges of dry woodland and downland.

When seen: All year round.

Breeds: Nest is well hidden on the ground. 3-4 eggs.

Voice: Varied calls, unlike Skylark's. Song – notes repeated in short phrases, each one descending – *klooklookloo; tlee tlee tlee tlee; lu-lu-lu-lu, deedl-eedl-eedl,* etc.

Feeding: Inconspicuously on the ground.

Flight: Broad wings, undulating action – more like Crested Lark than Skylark.

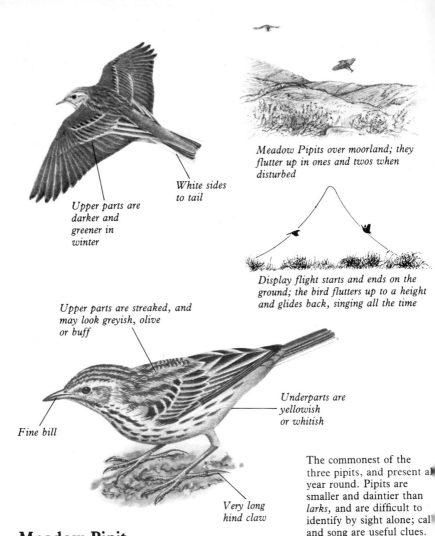

Meadow Pipits over moorland; they flutter up in ones and twos when disturbed

White sides to tail

Upper parts are darker and greener in winter

Display flight starts and ends on the ground; the bird flutters up to a height and glides back, singing all the time

Upper parts are streaked, and may look greyish, olive or buff

Underparts are yellowish or whitish

Fine bill

Very long hind claw

The commonest of the three pipits, and present all year round. Pipits are smaller and daintier than *larks*, and are difficult to identify by sight alone; call and song are useful clues.

Meadow Pipit

Anthus pratensis   14.5cm/5¾"
Habitat: Damp or dry moorland; heaths, dunes or saltmarshes.
When seen: All year round.
Breeds: Nests on the ground. 2 broods. 4-5 eggs.
Voice: Typically a thin, high *pseep*, often tripled. Song in display flight is prolonged: a series of *chip chip, swee swee*, etc. ending in a tinkling trill.
Feeding: Takes insects, spiders, seeds, etc. from the ground, walking about slowly with occasional short dashes or leaps after flies.
Flight: Undulating with bursts of wing-beats; may be fluttery over long distances.

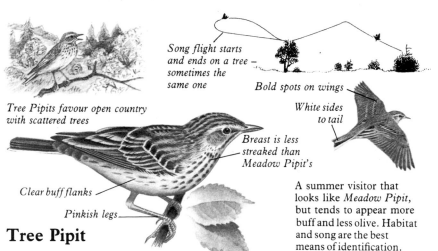

Song flight starts and ends on a tree – sometimes the same one

Tree Pipits favour open country with scattered trees

Bold spots on wings

White sides to tail

Breast is less streaked than Meadow Pipit's

Clear buff flanks

Pinkish legs

A summer visitor that looks like *Meadow Pipit*, but tends to appear more buff and less olive. Habitat and song are the best means of identification.

Tree Pipit

Anthus trivialis   15cm/6"

Habitat: Dry heaths with trees, woodland clearings, plantations, deciduous woods.
When seen: From April to September.
Breeds: Nest is well concealed on the ground. 4-6 eggs.
Voice: A hissing *teeze*. Song in flight has rolling *sirro sirro sirro* notes and final plaintive *swee-a see-er see-er* as bird drops back to perch.
Feeding: As Meadow Pipit. **Flight:** Like Meadow Pipit but a little stronger.

Song flight starts and ends on a rock or the ground

Rock Pipits on a rocky beach – this bird's habitat is a good clue to its identity

Dull grey-brown or olive back and head

Outer tail feathers are pale grey – not white

Olive-yellow under-parts

Dark legs

Rock Pipit

Anthus spinoletta   16.5cm/6½"

Looks like a larger, darker version of the *Meadow Pipit* with a slightly different call. Looks duller, greyer above and more olive beneath than *Skylark* or other pipits.

Habitat: Rocky seashores, cliffs; saltmarshes in winter.
When seen: All year round.
Breeds: Nests on the ground or in a cleft in rocks.
Voice: Call is *fist*, stronger than Meadow Pipit's and song is louder.
Feeding: As Meadow Pipit but often on seaweed or beaches.
Flight: As Meadow Pipit, but stronger. Similar song flight.

Song is usually delivered from a bush or hedge; note the bird's upright stance

Low, flitting flight is usually over short distances only

Dunnocks feeding in a garden; they hop quietly about on the ground

Back is richly marked with black and brown

Slender bill (unlike sparrows')

Typical crouched stance of a feeding bird

Grey face and breast

Dark streaks on flanks

Sides of breast have an orange tinge

Orange legs may be conspicuous

A small, quiet, unobtrusive bird, common in suburban gardens, parks, woodland and wild heathland alike. There is little plumage variation.

Dunnock

Prunella modularis   14.5cm/5¾"
Habitat: Hedgerows, woods, copses, heaths, scrub, parks and well-vegetated gardens.
When seen: All year round.
Breeds: Builds a neat nest lined with hair in a hedge or bush. 2 or 3 broods. 4-5 eggs.
Voice: A shrill, piping *tseep*; the song is a slightly flat, jingling warble, without the trills or power of the Wren.
Feeding: Creeps about hedge bottoms, under bushes, etc. with short hops, searching for insects, spiders, etc.
Flight: Rarely seen except for low, flitting flights from bush to bush.

Flies swiftly and straight, but only for short distances; rapid, whirring wing action is characteristic

Song is loud and strident – especially for such a small bird

A Wren at its nest in the undergrowth at the base of a hedge

Pale stripe over eye

Tail is often cocked

Barred wings and flanks are more strongly marked on some island races

Colour overall appears rusty-brown

A tiny, rotund bird with a slender bill, short round body and a cocked tail. A busy, active bird which is very common and easy to recognise. It often creeps about in dense, tangled vegetation.

Wren

Troglodytes troglodytes   9.5cm/3¾"

Habitat: All kinds of woodland, heaths, moors, cliffs, parks, gardens.
When seen: All year round.
Breeds: A neat nest with a side entrance is built amongst roots or in holes or crevices in a shed or other building. 2 broods. 5-6 eggs.
Voice: Harsh *chit chit, chititrrrr-rrr,* etc. Song is a loud, strident warbling with characteristic trills included.
Feeding: Explores all kinds of undergrowth in search of insects and spiders.
Flight: Short whirring flights, usually staying low.

Uniform olive-brown above

Flies with quick whirring wing action

Upper parts are brown with pale spots

Lacks red on breast

Underparts are buff with brown mottles

JUVENILE

Robin singing in a wood; this bird is also common in suburban gardens

Rounded head

Slender bill

Perky action on ground when searching for worms and insects

Orange face and breast have a bluish edge

A familiar bird, identified by its upright stance with wings drooped and tail depressed; also by its rounded head and slender bill. Spotted juvenile has the same shape and character as the adult.

Robin

Erithacus rubecula 14cm/5½"
Habitat: Deciduous and mixed woodland, plantations, parks, gardens and hedgerows.
When seen: All year round.
Breeds: Nest is well hidden in a bank, hedge, ivy, etc. 2 or 3 broods. 5-7 eggs.
Voice: Short sharp *tic, tic-ic*, etc. Song is a melodious, leisurely warbling, rich and full in spring, more melancholy in autumn with notes fading away.
Feeding: Searches the ground for worms, insects, etc., also for berries and seeds.
Flight: A fairly quick, whirring or flitting action.

Black eye in pale eye-ring

Rump and tail are rufous

Buff under-parts

Bright white forehead

♀

Pale brown back

♂

Blue-grey back

Intensely black face and throat

Perched birds often shiver their tails up and down

Dark centre to tail

Under-parts are orange or buff

A colourful but elusive bird of old woodlands. Song is a useful means of locating the male, often in a tree-top, or well concealed. Behaviour is *Robin-like.*

Redstart

Phoenicurus phoenicurus   14cm/5½"

Habitat: Parks, heaths with scattered trees, oak or mixed woods, some woodland edges.
When seen: From April to September.
Breeds: Nests in a hole in a wall or tree. 2 broods. 5-7 eggs.
Voice: *Whee-tic tic, wheet.* Song is a short warble with liquid and jarring notes.
Feeding: Flits through foliage after flies; short forays to the ground for insects.
Flight: Like Robin.

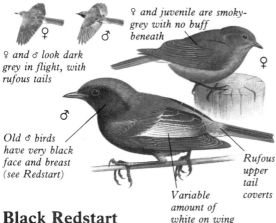

♀ and juvenile are smoky-grey with no buff beneath

♀ and ♂ look dark grey in flight, with rufous tails

♀

♂

Old ♂ birds have very black face and breast (see Redstart)

Rufous upper tail coverts

Variable amount of white on wing

Black Redstarts frequent derelict buildings, industrial sites and dumps

In character, resembles a *Redstart* or a slim *Robin* but its habitat is quite different and it is **rare in Britain.** Early morning song is useful for location.

Black Redstart

Phoenicurus ochruros   14cm/5½"

Habitat: Urban and industrial areas, crags, cliffs, and rocky shores.
When seen: All year round, although rare in Britain.
Breeds: Nests on ledges of buildings, holes in walls or rocks. 2 broods. 4-5 eggs.
Voice: *Tsee-tuctuc.* Song is a warble combined with odd rattling sounds.
Feeding: Like Redstart, but feeds on the ground much more.
Flight: Like Robin.

Pale stripe over eye

♂

Black face patch

♀

White patches at base of tail

♀

Scaly pattern on back of both ♀ and ♂

White on sides of tail (♂ too)

Peach, buff or pale yellow chin and breast

Whinchats usually perch in conspicuous places

A small, nervous bird which gives repeated calls when alarmed. The male is more contrasted than the female but the pale stripe over the eye is distinctive on both, as is the scaly pattern on the upper parts.

Whinchat

Saxicola rubetra   12.5cm/5"
Habitat: Heaths, commonland, waste ground and moors with scrub, bracken, etc.
When seen: From April to September.
Breeds: Nest is well hidden on the ground. 2 broods. 5-6 eggs.
Voice: *Teu tic-tic*, etc. – a short whistle combined with ticking notes. Variable song.
Feeding: Drops to the ground from its perch to take insects, spiders, etc.
Flight: Low over the ground and rather jerky.

♀

Dark brown upper parts

♀

Blackish head and black chin

♂

Large white neck patch

No white on tail (see Whinchat)

Male is duller in winter

White above black tail

Orange breast (♀ and ♂)

Stonechat on gorse above a rocky bay; also seen perched on overhead wires

Similar in behaviour to *Whinchat*, but is more erect. The upper and underparts are darker and there is no pale stripe above the eye.

Stonechat

Saxicola torquata   12.5cm/5"
Habitat: Like Whinchat, but often where there is more gorse.
When seen: All year round, unlike Whinchat.
Breeds: As Whinchat.
Voice: *Wee-tac-tac*; louder than Whinchat. Song is heard less often.
Feeding: Much like Whinchat.
Flight: Similar to Whinchat, but has a more whirring action.

White rump and black 'T' shape on tail are obvious in flight in all seasons, both ♂ and ♀

♀

♂

Head is browner than ♂'s – no black

Grey-brown back

Brown wings

♀

SPRING, SUMMER

Wheatears are often seen standing in an erect stance on walls, wires, boulders, etc.

Back is brown and speckled

Buff edges to wing and tail feathers

JUVENILE, SUMMER

♂

Upper parts are clean grey (see Whinchat)

Black patch through eye

Pale chin

Blackish wings

Buff underparts

SPRING, SUMMER

An active bird that hops, flits and runs about on open ground chasing insects. The white rump and sides of the black-tipped tail are distinctive at all times. In autumn, both sexes are buff-brown with pale edges to their flight feathers.

Wheatear

Oenanthe oenanthe   14.5cm/5¾"
Habitat: Moorland with rocks and scree, marginal upland farmland with stone walls; downs and dunes; on passage, may be seen in fields, on golf courses, etc.
When seen: From March to October – one of our earliest summer visitors.
Breeds: Nest of grass, moss, feathers, etc. in hole in ground, wall, etc. 5-6 eggs.
Voice: *Chack, wheechakchak, wheet,* etc. Song is a mixed warble with grating notes.
Feeding: Chases insects on the ground; leaps and flies up to catch flies in the air.
Flight: Fast and direct – jerky over short distances.

Strong purple and green gloss

Largely yellow bill

Sings with puffy throat and fluttering, drooped wings

SUMMER

Stout body

Short tail

Pointed, triangular wings

Starlings are common in city parks; whilst walking, they probe the ground for food with a more continuous action than the Blackbird's

JUVENILE

Pale throat

Streaked breast

Dark, drab brown plumage

Short, square tail

WINTER

Long, pointed bill

Plumage is heavily marked with buff and white speckling but still looks black at a distance

Orange edges to wing feathers

Reddish legs

Bold, noisy bird often seen at bird feeders or on lawns. Behaviour is noisy and aggressive. The jaunty walk, leaping hop or run, pointed bill, short square tail and glossy plumage are very distinctive.

Starling

Sturnus vulgaris   22cm/8½"
Habitat: Woods, marshes, moors, farmland, parks, gardens, suburbs.
When seen: All year round.
Breeds: In all sorts of holes in trees, cliffs, walls and buildings. 4-7 eggs.
Voice: *Tcheer, tic tic, peuw,* etc. Song is a varied mixture of warbles, trills, rattles and whistles delivered with typically puffed-out throat and flicking wings.
Feeding: Probes for worms, beetles, grubs, etc. in fields and lawns. Takes scraps.
Flight: Fast and direct; flocks form dense packs, lines and 'snakes', capable of rapid integrated manoeuvres.

♂

Low, direct, fast flight over short distances, often jerking tail upwards

Broad wings

Blackbirds feeding on the ground, with another singing in a tree

JUVENILE

Back and head are more rufous than ♀ Blackbird's

Spotted breast

Darker overall than Song Thrush; never pale buff beneath

Dark brown plumage

♀

Bill is yellow at base, or all dark

Throat is pale and streaked

Yellow eye-ring

♂

Yellow bill

Long tail (see Starling)

All-black plumage with little gloss

A very common bird of gardens and parkland. Bold and aggressive. An exceptional songster. Juveniles should not be confused with *Song Thrush*.

Blackbird

Turdus merula   25cm/10″
Habitat: Woodland, farmland, gardens, parks, heaths, etc.
When seen: All year round.
Breeds: Bulky nest in a bush or hedge lined with grass. 2 or 3 broods. 3-5 eggs.
Voice: *Tchook, pinkpink pink* and a loud, strident, rattle. Song is rich and throaty but with most phrases petering out – not repetitive (see Song Thrush).
Feeding: Probes noisily amongst grass, leaf litter, etc. for worms, insects and grubs. Takes berries from bushes and hedges.
Flight: Rather weak and flicking; nervous and hesitant for a bird of its size.

Bright buff under-wing

JUVENILE

Spots on underparts are smaller than those on adult

Loud, repetitive song is delivered from a high perch, such as a chimney pot

Looks alert when feeding, often with head tilted to one side

Upper parts are warm olive brown (paler than those of juvenile Blackbird)

Underparts are bright buff with dark brown spots in streaks

Belly can look silky white

Resembles the *Blackbird* in behaviour and habitat, but is much smaller and its upper parts are much paler and more olive than those of the *young Blackbird*, with which it might be confused. A fine songster.

Song Thrush

Turdus philomelos   23cm/9″
Habitat: Woods and hedges, also frequents parks and suburban gardens.
When seen: All year round.
Breeds: Nest like Blackbird's but has mud lining; in hedge, ivy, etc. 2-3 broods. 4-5 eg
Voice: *Sip, stip* and dry, harsh alarm rattle. Song is loud and clear, more varied than Mistle Thrush's but, unlike Blackbird, each phrase is repeated 3 or 4 times.
Feeding: Probes for worms, insects, etc. like Blackbird. Smashes snails on stones.
Flight: Hesitant, weak and flitting like Blackbird.

White
under-wing

Large, pale
rump

White sides to tail

Loud, far-carrying song is delivered
from the top of a tree

JUVENILE

Pale and
yellowish
overall

Larger and longer than Song Thrush;
hops boldly when feeding

Small head
in relation
to body

Upper parts are paler
and greyer than those
of Song Thrush

Underparts are
pale buff with
round, blackish
spots (less
aligned than
those of Song Thrush)

Pale edges to
wing feathers

A bold elongated bird on
the ground with a strong
hop. Larger and paler than
Blackbird and paler, greyer
and larger than *Song
Thrush.*

Mistle Thrush

Turdus viscivorus   27cm/10½"
Habitat: Woods and woodland edges, heaths, moors, parks and farmland.
When seen: All year round.
Breeds: Large nest is often high up in an open tree. 2 broods. 3-5 eggs.
Voice: Harsh, churring rattle, almost a hiss. Song is of fine, throaty quality; short
phrases repeated often. Less varied than Blackbird, more limited than Song Thrush.
Feeding: More in open than Blackbird, bolder than Song Thrush. Also takes berries.
Flight: Stronger than other thrushes, often high, with long bounding undulations.

Dark cheek patch

Pale stripe over eye and under cheek

Reddish under-wing (see Song Thrush)

Upper parts are darker than those of Song Thrush

Underparts are whiter and more streaked than Song Thrush's

A flock of Redwings and Fieldfares feeding in a field in winter

Rufous flanks

A winter visitor often found in mixed loose flocks with *Fieldfares*. Slightly smaller than Song Thrush.

Redwing

Turdus iliacus   21cm/8¼"
Habitat: Open country, farmland, hedges, parks; visits lawns, gardens in cold weather.
When seen: From October to April.
Breeds: A very few breed in Scotland. 5-6 eggs.
Voice: Flight note is a distinctive, high *seee*. Has a rattling alarm call.
Feeding: In winter, feeds in flocks in fields. Takes worms, grubs, berries.
Flight: Over long distances, fairly slow with bouts of flickering wing-beats.

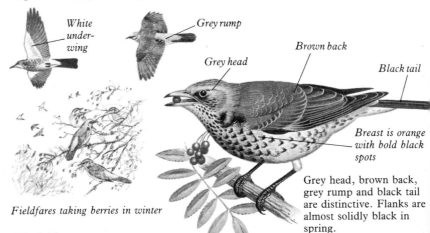

White under-wing

Grey rump

Brown back

Grey head

Black tail

Breast is orange with bold black spots

Fieldfares taking berries in winter

Grey head, brown back, grey rump and black tail are distinctive. Flanks are almost solidly black in spring.

Fieldfare

Turdus pilaris   25cm/10"
Habitat: As Redwing but less often in parks and gardens, more often in upland fields.
When seen: From October to April.
Voice: Loud, rattling *chack-chack-chack* and a nasal *ee-eep*.
Feeding: Like Redwing. Often in evenly dispersed flocks across meadows.
Flight: Like Mistle Thrush; stronger than Redwing. Frequently in large flocks.

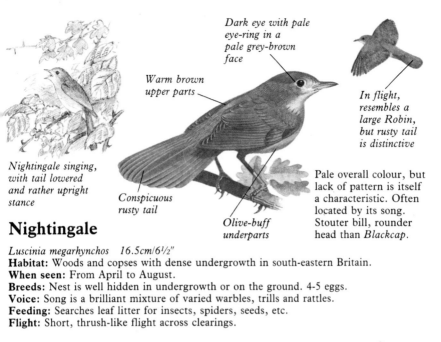

Dark eye with pale eye-ring in a pale grey-brown face

Warm brown upper parts

In flight, resembles a large Robin, but rusty tail is distinctive

Nightingale singing, with tail lowered and rather upright stance

Conspicuous rusty tail

Olive-buff underparts

Pale overall colour, but lack of pattern is itself a characteristic. Often located by its song. Stouter bill, rounder head than *Blackcap*.

Nightingale

Luscinia megarhynchos   16.5cm/6½"
Habitat: Woods and copses with dense undergrowth in south-eastern Britain.
When seen: From April to August.
Breeds: Nest is well hidden in undergrowth or on the ground. 4-5 eggs.
Voice: Song is a brilliant mixture of varied warbles, trills and rattles.
Feeding: Searches leaf litter for insects, spiders, seeds, etc.
Flight: Short, thrush-like flight across clearings.

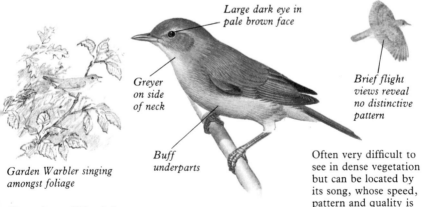

Large dark eye in pale brown face

Greyer on side of neck

Brief flight views reveal no distinctive pattern

Buff underparts

Often very difficult to see in dense vegetation but can be located by its song, whose speed, pattern and quality is unlike any other bird's.

Garden Warbler singing amongst foliage

Garden Warbler

Sylvia borin   13cm/5¼"
Habitat: Deciduous woods, hedges with tall trees and in thick undergrowth.
When seen: From April to September.
Breeds: The flimsy nest is built in a hedge or bush. 4-5 eggs.
Voice: Soft *tac, chuff chuff*, etc. Rich, mellow song, rather similar to Blackcap's.
Feeding: Takes insects and in autumn also takes berries.
Flight: A weak, flitting action.

Slightly jerky, flitting flight

♂

Tail is slim and fairly long

Sylvia warblers are larger and heavier in their actions than Phylloscopus warblers and lack green coloration

Blackcap singing from deep inside an overgrown thicket

Black forehead and cap

Grey lores and chin

♂

Grey-brown upper parts

Dull, rufous-brown cap

♀

Browner than ♂

Greyish, unmarked underparts

A grey or brown warbler which inhabits woods and thickets. Often first revealed by its song or call. Compare with the more contrasted *Marsh Tit*.

Blackcap

Sylvia atricapilla   14cm/5½"
Habitat: Open woodland with plentiful undergrowth, also old overgrown hedges.
When seen: From April to September; a few in parks and gardens in winter.
Breeds: Builds a neat nest of grasses, etc. in a bush or hedge. 4-5 eggs.
Voice: *Tack-tack.* Song is similar to Garden Warbler's but starts lower and has an abrupt outburst of rich, throaty warbling; shorter than Nightingale's or thrushes'.
Feeding: Keeps in cover, searching foliage for insects. Takes berries in autumn. During the winter months may be seen in gardens with bird-tables and shrubs.
Flight: Typical low, flitting flight of warblers; rarely flies any distance.

Browner head than ♂

♀

Longish, slim tail

Dark tail has white sides

Warm brown upper parts

Grey head

Pale eye

♂

Rusty edges to wing feathers

Pale, straw-coloured legs

White throat

Pinkish underparts

Whitethroat singing in brambles

A jaunty bird, characterised by its long, 'loose', white-sided tail, pure white chin and throat and overall rufous appearance.

Whitethroat

Sylvia communis 14cm/5½"

Habitat: Rough heaths, waste ground, woodland edges and hedgerows.
When seen: From April to September.
Breeds: Nest is well hidden in undergrowth. 2 broods. 4-5 eggs.
Voice: Soft, scolding *charr, tack-tack, wheet-wheet;* scratchy, warbling song.
Feeding: Takes insects, spiders and berries.
Flight: Low and flicking, with a 'loose' tail. Song flight has a steep climb with floppy wing action, then a dive back to a bush.

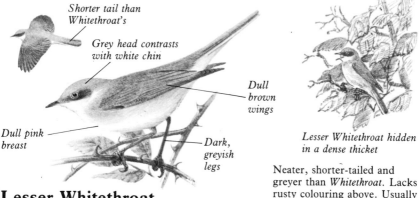

Shorter tail than Whitethroat's

Grey head contrasts with white chin

Dull brown wings

Dull pink breast

Dark, greyish legs

Lesser Whitethroat hidden in a dense thicket

Neater, shorter-tailed and greyer than *Whitethroat.* Lacks rusty colouring above. Usually looks clean and smart.

Lesser Whitethroat

Sylvia curruca 13cm/5¼"

Habitat: Dense thickets, old overgrown hedges, etc.
When seen: From April to September. In autumn, seen in areas where none breed.
Breeds: Nest is well hidden in a bush. 4-6 eggs.
Voice: *Tac;* thinner than Blackcap's. Short warble ends with rattling *chikikikikikik.*
Feeding: Like Whitethroat: especially fond of honeysuckle berries.
Flight: Shorter tail gives a tidier appearance than Whitethroat.

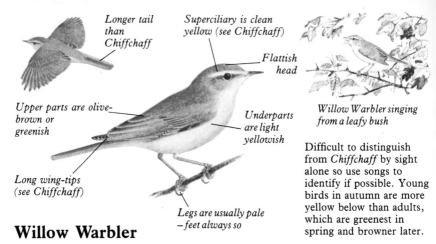

Longer tail than Chiffchaff

Superciliary is clean yellow (see Chiffchaff)

Flattish head

Upper parts are olive-brown or greenish

Underparts are light yellowish

Long wing-tips (see Chiffchaff)

Legs are usually pale – feet always so

Willow Warbler singing from a leafy bush

Willow Warbler

Difficult to distinguish from *Chiffchaff* by sight alone so use songs to identify if possible. Young birds in autumn are more yellow below than adults, which are greenest in spring and browner later.

Phylloscopus trochilus 11cm/4¼"
Habitat: Bushy commons, hedges and deciduous woods, trees near water.
When seen: From April to September. Autumn migrants outside breeding areas.
Breeds: Builds a domed nest well hidden on the ground. 6-7 eggs.
Voice: *Hoo-eet.* Song is a sweet, flowing warble descending the scale.
Feeding: Takes insects etc. from foliage. Quicker actions than those of Sylvia warblers.
Flight: Quick, light, nervous flitting.

Short tail

Superciliary is thin and diffuse

Round head (see Willow Warbler)

Short wing-tips (see Willow Warbler)

Eye-ring is well defined

Legs are very dark and strikingly thin

Underparts are dull and pale

Chiffchaff's distinctive song is delivered from a high perch

Chiffchaff

Fractionally smaller, less sleek and a bit duller than *Willow Warbler.* Flicks tail and wings more constantly. Young birds are yellow beneath in autumn.

Phylloscopus collybita 11cm/4¼"
Habitat: Usually more restricted to woodland, in taller trees than Willow Warbler.
When seen: From March to September, although a few are seen in winter.
Breeds: Builds a rounded nest just above ground level. 6 eggs.
Voice: *Hweet,* just less disyllabic than Willow Warbler. Song is a sequence of 3 or 4 single notes – *chi-chew-chew-chee-chif-chif-chee-chew,* etc.
Feeding and Flight: Like Willow Warbler.

Long wings; a bit like a flycatcher in flight

White belly may be obvious in flight

Sometimes sings from exposed perch low down; also flits restlessly about in tree canopy

Wood Warbler at its nest on the woodland floor

Broad yellow stripe over eye is more obvious than in Willow Warbler

Upper parts are a clearer green than in other warblers

Brown wing-feathers are neatly edged with yellow

Long wing-tips are often drooped

Chin and throat are pale yellow, often blending into white underparts (but may contrast with white more sharply)

A slightly larger and stouter bird than either Willow Warbler or Chiffchaff. Can often be located by its song.

Legs are pale orange-brown

Belly is more silvery white than Willow Warbler's

Wood Warbler

Phylloscopus sibilatrix 12.5cm/5"

Habitat: Mature woods of oak, beech, larch, etc. with little undergrowth, but plenty of leaf litter. Mostly in the North and West.

When seen: From April to August. Migrants very rare away from breeding sites.

Breeds: A domed nest is well concealed on the woodland floor. 5-7 eggs.

Voice: A loud, plaintive *pew*. Song is a sharp note which accelerates into a shrill trill – *tip tip tip tiptrreeeeee*. Also *pew* note repeated in a regular sequence.

Feeding: Restless flitting through the tree canopy searching for flies, etc.

Flight: Flight is stronger and wings are longer than Willow Warbler's.

103

In flight, wings are drooped and tail is spread

Upper parts are warm brown

Long bill

Unmarked plumage is a good clue

Long tail

Rufous rump

Whitish throat

Buff underparts

Birds in reeds, sidling up vertical stems and singing

Slightly larger, slimmer and more elongated than *Sedge Warbler*, with a flatter forehead, longer bill and tail.

Reed Warbler

Acrocephalus scirpaceus   12.5cm/5"

Habitat: Reedbeds in shallow water, sedges, some in willows, etc.
When seen: From April to September.
Breeds: Neat nest of grass, reeds, etc. is woven around reed stems. 3-5 eggs.
Voice: *Churr*. Song is a rhythmic sequence of whistles and churrs with many repetitions.
Feeding: Takes insects from reed stems and adjacent bushes.
Flight: Fairly quick and direct; often seen flitting short distances.

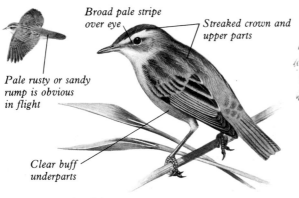

Broad pale stripe over eye

Streaked crown and upper parts

Pale rusty or sandy rump is obvious in flight

Clear buff underparts

Sedge Warblers often sing from tangled undergrowth

Habitat is similar to *Reed Warbler's;* song is similar but plumage, especially pale stripe over eye, is distinctive; a more excitable bird.

Sedge Warbler

Acrocephalus schoenobaenus   12.5cm/5"

Habitat: Often more mixed than that of Reed Warbler – reeds, tall herbs, low willows.
When seen: From April to September.
Breeds: The solidly-constructed nest is built in low undergrowth. 5-6 eggs.
Voice: *Tuc*, rattling calls. Song is more varied, less repetitive than Reed Warbler's.
Feeding: Takes insects etc. from low vegetation, often in deep cover.
Flight: Usually low and flitting but also has a short, high, whirring song flight.

Usually seen flying out in short circuits to catch aerial insects

Crown and breast are softly streaked

Upper parts are dull brown

Pale edges on wing feathers

Underside is pale grey-buff

Alert, perched bird, ready to fly out to catch insects

Upright stance, alert expression and soft, pale colouring give very distinct character, despite lack of pattern.

Spotted Flycatcher

Muscicapa striata   14cm/5½"
Habitat: Woodland, parks, gardens, tennis courts, etc.
When seen: From May to September – a late arrival in spring.
Breeds: Nest is built in ivy on walls or in holes in trees. 4-5 eggs.
Voice: *Tsit* and *tee-tucc.* Short variable song is unobtrusive, sometimes warbling.
Feeding: Usually takes aerial insects but sometimes takes insects from the ground.
Flight: Stronger than that of warblers – fly-catching sallies are very characteristic.

♂

Large white area

White on forehead

♂

♀

Upper parts are blackish

Brown upper parts

Pied Flycatchers often nest in nest-boxes

White underparts

Inconspicuous, despite striking pattern; often hard to see in trees but song helps location. A neat bird, smaller than *Robin.*

Pied Flycatcher

Ficedula hypoleuca   12.5cm/5"
Habitat: Usually woodland, especially oak, and often near streams.
When seen: From April to September. Migrants on east coast in autumn.
Breeds: Builds nest in natural holes or nest-boxes. 5-8 eggs.
Voice: *Whit, wheet.* Song is hesitant compared with that of most warblers.
Feeding: More restricted to the tree canopy than Spotted Flycatcher.
Flight: Similar to Spotted Flycatcher; does not often return to same perch.

Blue tail

Details hard to see in flight

Juvenile has a yellower head than adult

JUVENILE

Blue Tits often use nest-boxes

Bright blue cap surrounded by white

Green back

Dark eye-stripe, chin and borders to white cheeks

Dark streak on belly

Blue wings with white bar

Yellow underparts

A familiar, acrobatic, entertaining bird. Bold and lively, with distinctive bright colouring.

Blue Tit

Parus caeruleus   11.5cm/4½″

Habitat: Woodland of all kinds, plantations, parks, gardens.

When seen: All year round. Numbers may increase greatly in autumn and winter.

Breeds: Nests in a natural hole in a tree, a wall, in a nest-box, etc. 7-14 eggs.

Voice: *Tsee; tsee tsee tsee chrrrr; tseetseechuchuchuchuch*, etc., a variety of high, thin notes, churrs and trills.

Feeding: Active, acrobatic, opportunist feeder, searching for insects, caterpillars, spiders, etc. Fond of fat, cheese and nuts from feeders.

Flight: Weak and flitting; a gliding 'butterfly' display flight.

White outer tail feathers are distinctive as bird flies away

White bar on bluish wings

Yellow on cheeks

Duller plumage than adult

JUVENILE

Great Tits and Blue Tits feeding at a bird-table in winter

Striking white cheeks

Black head

Green back

Obvious white edges to dark tertiary feathers

Black central stripe is broad on ♂, tapering away on belly of ♀

Yellow underparts

Familiar bird with a distinctive pattern; acrobatic in trees and on feeders. Also feeds on the ground beneath trees such as beech.

Great Tit

Parus major   14cm/5½"

Habitat: All kinds of woodland, parkland, hedges, gardens.
When seen: All year round.
Breeds: Nests in a hole in a tree or wall, nest-box, etc. 5-12 eggs.
Voice: Very varied repertoire. Calls *pink, tee-chu tee-chu tee-chu, chip chip chip, tcharr tcharr tcharr*, etc. Many notes are distinctly loud and strident.
Feeding: Acrobatic and lively after insects, spiders, buds, etc. On the ground more often than Blue Tit, searching leaf litter for nuts, berries, worms.
Flight: Bursts of rapid wing-beats giving undulating action.

Double wing-bars can be seen in flight and at rest

Coal Tits feeding on conifer seeds in a pinewood

Yellower cheeks and nape than adult

JUVENILE

Black crown

Oblong white patch on nape

Olive-brown or greyish upper parts with two pale bars on wings

White cheeks

Large black throat patch

Bright buff underparts

Agile and active; smaller than *Great Tit*, lacking bright yellow or blue on plumage; see *Marsh* and *Willow Tits*. White patch on nape is diagnostic.

Coal Tit

Parus ater   11.5cm/4½"
Habitat: Mixed, deciduous or coniferous woods, parks.
When seen: All year round.
Breeds: Nests in a hole in a tree, a wall or the ground. 8-11 eggs.
Voice: Plaintive, ringing quality of call is distinctive. Thin *tsew, tsee, tsee*, etc., and repetitive *seeto seeto seeto* with strong carrying power.
Feeding: Much like Great Tit. Often on ground beneath beech trees in autumn, amongst foliage in summer. Very active, restless and energetic.
Flight: Flitting flight like Blue Tit.

Black cap and chin are neater than Willow Tit's; pale cheeks extend less far back

Upper parts are grey-brown

Marsh Tits feeding on insects and grubs in a wood

Marsh Tit

Pale grey-buff underparts

Very like *Willow Tit*; best distinguished by its voice. See *Blackcap*.

Parus palustris   11.5cm/4½"
Habitat: Dry deciduous woods. Not often in gardens.
When seen: All year round.
Breeds: In a hole in a tree or wall. 6-8 eggs.
Voice: Distinctive loud, sharp, sudden *pitchew*. Also a buzzing *churr*, *chik-adeedeedee*, etc. Song is a simple, bubbling rattle *ship-ip-ip-ip-ip-ip-ip-ip*.
Feeding: Like other tits, but slower than Coal or Blue Tit. Often high in trees.
Flight: Like Blue Tit.

Black cap is duller than Marsh Tit's – goes further back over nape

Dull brown upper parts

Often has a light panel on wings

Pale cheeks are more extensive than Marsh Tit's

Willow Tits in a wet mixed woodland

Underparts are brighter than Marsh Tit's with more orange on flanks

Larger head and thicker neck than *Marsh Tit* – has a rounder shape.

Willow Tit

Parus montanus   11.5cm/4½"
Habitat: Like Marsh Tit but more often in damper mixed woods. Occasionally in gardens.
When seen: All year round.
Breeds: Excavates its own nest hole in a tree. 6-9 eggs.
Voice: High, thin notes and a distinctive nasal, buzzing *eez-eez-eez* or *chair chair chair*, deeper than Marsh Tit. Song is usually a clear *pew pew pew*.
Feeding and Flight: Like Marsh Tit, but frequently lower down.

Long tail is very distinctive in flight

Groups of Long-tailed Tits tend to cross open spaces one by one, not as a flock

Black stripes at side of crown join black nape

Tiny bill

Sides of head, nape and back are dull blackish; less pink than on adult

JUVENILE

Degree of pink on belly is variable

White crown

Black and pink upper parts

Black tail with white edges

Dull white face and breast

A tiny, rounded bird with a distinctively long tail, even on juveniles. Small flocks move steadily through trees or along hedges.

White edges to wing feathers

Long-tailed Tit

Aegithalos caudatus   14cm/5½" (7.5cm/3" being tail)
Habitat: Tall hedges, scrub, thickets, woodlands.
When seen: All year round.
Breeds: Exceptional domed nest covered with moss, lichen and cobwebs, and with a side entrance in a hedge or bush. 7-12 eggs.
Voice: Thin, high tuneless *zee-zee-zee*. Abrupt *tupp*, trilling *tsirrup*.
Feeding: Restless and active, searching foliage for caterpillars, spiders, etc.
Flight: Flitting flight with long trailing tail.

Two white bars on dark wings

Thin line of yellow edged with black on crown

Green upper parts

♀

Black patch

Goldcrests in a fir tree

Breeding ♂ has orange crest

Slight moustache

♂

Pale greenish-buff underparts

A tiny, restless bird, the size of a *Wren*, but shaped like a dumpy *warbler*. Juveniles lack colour on the crown.

Goldcrest

Regulus regulus   9cm/3½"
Habitat: Coniferous and mixed woodland, parks; bushy areas in winter.
When seen: All year round.
Breeds: Neat, tidy nest slung beneath spray of a conifer. 2 broods. 7-8 eggs.
Voice: Thin, high calls – *zee-zee-zee* etc. Song ends with a flourish – *tidldi-ee*.
Feeding: Takes tiny insects etc. from foliage.
Flight: Quick, flitting action.

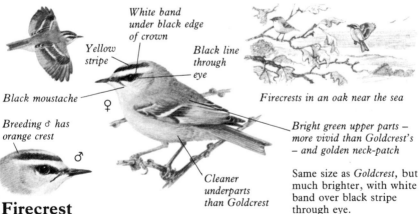

White band under black edge of crown

Yellow stripe

Black line through eye

Black moustache

♀

Firecrests in an oak near the sea

Breeding ♂ has orange crest

♂

Bright green upper parts – more vivid than Goldcrest's – and golden neck-patch

Cleaner underparts than Goldcrest

Same size as *Goldcrest*, but much brighter, with white band over black stripe through eye.

Firecrest

Regulus ignicapillus   9cm/3½"
Habitat: Parks and woodland. Breeds in spruce, maple, etc.
When seen: Mostly in spring and autumn; few breed and winter here.
Breeds: Much as Goldcrest.
Voice: Less thin than Goldcrest. Song is a very thin whistle with less pattern and no terminal flourish: simply speeds up at the end – *zee-e-e-ee-ee-eet*.
Feeding and Flight: As Goldcrest.

Dark red band behind eye

Grey crown

Pale streak over eye

Streaked above

Head pattern is less distinct in winter

♂

♀

♂

Black bib

Clean grey underparts

Upper parts are red-brown with dark streaks

House Sparrows gather near inhabited buildings

House Sparrow

A noisy, gregarious bird. Usually the most common species near habitation. May be duller than shown in city areas.

Passer domesticus   15cm/5¾"
Habitat: Near human habitation of all kinds. Flocks in fields in autumn and winter.
When seen: All year round.
Breeds: Builds an untidy nest in buildings, in trees, hedges, etc. 2-7 eggs.
Voice: *Chirps* and *cheeps,* often run together as a kind of song.
Feeding: Seeds, grain, scraps, insects; an opportunist with catholic tastes.
Flight: Direct and swift, bouncy over a distance.

Whitish collar

Squarish black spot on white cheek

Chocolate brown crown

Upper parts are less reddish than House Sparrow's

Black bill

Small black bib

Buffish underparts

Tree Sparrows in a country garden

Tree Sparrow

Smaller, neater and more compact than *House Sparrow.* Brown crown and black cheek spot are diagnostic.

Passer montanus   14cm/5½"
Habitat: Cultivated areas with trees. More rural than House Sparrow. Scarce in gardens.
When seen: All year round.
Breeds: A nest of dry grass in holes in old trees, nest-boxes. 2-7 eggs.
Voice: Similar to House Sparrow's but distinctive, hard *teck* in flight.
Feeding: Seeds, grain and insects. May join winter finch flocks in fields.
Flight: Like House Sparrow.

Green back

Bright yellow patches on tail

♂

Long wings with yellow streaks

Juvenile's plumage is browner than adult's, and is softly streaked, but still shows some yellow

JUVENILE

A flock of Greenfinches feeding in a field in winter

Yellow patches on wings and tail

♀ is duller than ♂

♀

Bluish patch on secondaries

♂

Large finch with a large head, stout pale bill and forked tail. Some are drab, but yellow patches are distinctive.

Bright yellow patches on wings and tail

Bright apple-green underparts

Greenfinch

Carduelis chloris   14cm/5½"
Habitat: Thick hedges, parks, scrub, woodland edges, suburbs.
When seen: All year round.
Breeds: A bulky nest is built in a bush or hedge. 2 broods. 4-6 eggs.
Voice: A rapid, metallic trill; a nasal *tsooee*. Song is a twittering trill with deep, buzzing *dzeee* and call notes intermixed.
Feeding: Seeds, grain, insects; forages in flocks during winter. Visits bird-tables.
Flight: Strong and quick, rather undulating. Spring song flight has slower, wavy beats of outstretched wings.

Do not confuse with *Brambling*

Orange (not white) shoulder patch

White (not green) rump

♀

WINTER

Similar to *Chaffinch*, but *Brambling* is not seen in the summer

Flocks of Chaffinches feed on grain, spiders, etc. in fields during the winter

White shoulder patch, wing-bar and sides of tail are especially clear in flight

♀

♀ is duller and browner than ♂, and in winter ♂ resembles ♀ in colouring

Blue-grey crown and nape

Black patch above grey bill

♂

Wing and tail patches are distinctive

Pink face and breast (see Bullfinch)

Brown back

Green rump

SUMMER

White shoulder

Broad white shoulder patch, white wing-bar and sides of tail are always distinctive. Has a slimmer, longer tail than *Greenfinch* or *sparrows*.

Chaffinch

Fringilla coelebs   15cm/6"
Habitat: Woodland of all sorts, plantations, parks, gardens, farmland.
When seen: All year round.
Breeds: Builds a neat, mossy nest in the fork of a bush or tree. 4-5 eggs.
Voice: Loud *chwink-chwink;* clear, strident *wheet* in spring; short *tsup tsup* in flight.
Song is loud and bright with a metallic, rattling quality and a terminal flourish – *chip chip chip, cherry-erry-erry – chipit-cheweeoo*, etc.
Feeding: Searches foliage for caterpillars; in leaf litter for berries, seeds, worms, grain, etc; takes bread, scraps.
Flight: Bounding flight with bursts of rapid wing-beats.

Brownish back

♀

White rump and wing-bars are especially distinctive in flight

♂

Grey back

Bullfinches feeding on buds and blossom

JUVENILE

Browner plumage than adults', with no black on head

Head pattern is like that of ♂

♀

Black cap, face and bill

♂

Pinkish-brown underparts

Deep pink underside (brighter than Chaffinch's)

Whitish bar on black wing

Black tail

Quiet, secretive finch of woods and hedgerows. Short but stout bill, soft silky plumage, pale wing-bar and white rump are diagnostic.

Bullfinch

Pyrrhula pyrrhula   14.5cm/5¾"
Habitat: Deciduous woods, orchards, gardens, thickets, hedgerows.
When seen: All year round.
Breeds: Builds a nest of twigs and roots in a bush, bramble, etc.
2 broods. 4-6 eggs.
Voice: Poor, creaky song. Usual call is low, clear, piping whistle – *peee* or *piuw*.
Feeding: Takes buds and blossom, insects, seeds, berries. Less often on ground than other finches and usually taking softer food.
Flight: Short, flitting flights from bush to bush.

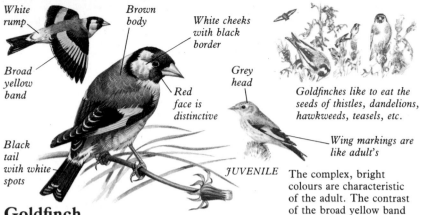

White rump

Brown body

White cheeks with black border

Broad yellow band

Red face is distinctive

Grey head

Goldfinches like to eat the seeds of thistles, dandelions, hawkweeds, teasels, etc.

Wing markings are like adult's

Black tail with white spots

JUVENILE The complex, bright colours are characteristic of the adult. The contrast of the broad yellow band on the black wing is unique.

Goldfinch

Carduelis carduelis 12cm/4¾"
Habitat: Light woodland, gardens with trees, parks, avenues, weedy areas.
When seen: All year round.
Breeds: Neat, round nest near the end of a tree branch. 2 broods. 5-6 eggs.
Voice: Rippling twitter – *tswit-wit-wit*, etc. Song has liquid warbles.
Feeding: Vegetable matter, especially seeds. Often feeds in small flocks.
Flight: Dancing, undulating action, lighter than that of other finches.

♂

Bright brown back with no streaks

Red forehead and breast

♂

Head is browner than ♂'s

♀

White streaks on blackish wings show in flight

Large flocks gather in autumn and winter to forage on waste ground

White sides to tail

SPRING

Whitish underparts contrast with upper parts

Small, colourful finch with bounding flight. Cheerful, singing groups form in late winter and spring. See *Redpoll*.

Linnet

Back is slightly streaked

Acanthis cannabina 13cm/5¼"
Habitat: Heaths, woodland edges, gorsy areas, hedgerows; fields, saltmarsh in winter.
When seen: All year round.
Breeds: Neat, small nest lined with hair and thistledown. 4-6 eggs.
Voice: Rapid, twittering *chich-ich-ich-ich* in flight; *tseow* etc. Twittering song.
Feeding: Takes seeds and vegetable matter from on or near ground.
Flight: Rapid, undulating flight is lighter than Greenfinch's.

LESSER REDPOLL

♂ has pink breast in spring

Streaked brown and buff

Buff or whitish wing-bars

Red forehead

Yellow bill

Small black bib

MEALY REDPOLL

Streaked flanks

Redpolls in a birch tree

Small, agile, slender finch with forked tail and small bill. Two forms of the same species: the Mealy is slightly larger, slightly paler and has whiter wing-bars than the Lesser.

Redpoll

Acanthis flammea   12cm/4¾"
Habitat: Bushy heaths, open woods; birchwoods, riverside alders, etc. in winter.
When seen: Lesser Redpoll all year round. Mealy Redpoll is a scarce winter visitor.
Breeds: Nests in a bush or tree. 4-6 eggs.
Voice: Nasal *tswee;* rapid, hard trill *chuch-uch-uch-uch;* song is similar with trills.
Feeding: Takes much of its food from trees (unlike Linnet); also seeds from ground.
Flight: Quicker, more energetic than Linnet.

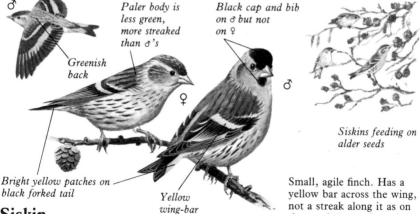

Paler body is less green, more streaked than ♂'s

Greenish back

Black cap and bib on ♂ but not on ♀

♀

♂

Siskins feeding on alder seeds

Bright yellow patches on black forked tail

Yellow wing-bar

Small, agile finch. Has a yellow bar across the wing, not a streak along it as on the much larger *Greenfinch*.

Siskin

Carduelis spinus   12cm/4¾"
Habitat: Usually conifers in summer; like Redpoll in winter.
When seen: All year round, but most familiar in winter in the South.
Breeds: High in a tree. 2 broods. 4-5 eggs.
Voice: Flight calls are more chattering than Redpoll's, plus squeaky *styee, sy-een,* etc.
Feeding: Seeds of larch, alder, birch, spruce, etc. Often in flocks with Redpoll.
Flight: Fast and bounding, bursting from tree-tops in tight flocks.

♀

Chestnut rump is distinctive in flight on both sexes

♂

Posture when singing

♂

A flock of Yellowhammers foraging on wasteland in winter

Dark streaks on head

♂

Back is chestnut, buff and black

♀ is duller than ♂ with paler and less extensive areas of yellow

♀

Chestnut on sides of breast and flanks

Typical bunting shape with a small, pointed head and bill and rather long, loosely held tail. The yellow of the male is at its most brilliant in spring.

White on black tail

Heavily streaked underparts

Yellowhammer

Emberiza citrinella   16.5cm/6½"
Habitat: Bushy commons, hedgerows with tall trees, bushy hillsides, fields.
When seen: All year round.
Breeds: Nests in banks, under hedges, etc. 2 or 3 broods. 3-5 eggs.
Voice: Thin, metallic *tsip, chik*. Song is a thin, wheezy rattling on one note with one or two longer notes at the end – *chipchipchipchipchipchip chee-oo*.
Feeding: Takes food almost entirely from the ground – insects, spiders, grain, etc.
Flight: Jerky flitting with a flicked tail.

118

♀

Large rufous area

Blackish outline
to reddish
cheeks

Stout
bill

White
sides to
tail are
distinctive
in flight

Upper side is
streaked black

♀

♂ in winter plumage

Longish,
untidy
black and
white tail

Black
head
and bib
in spring

The male has less black on
its head in winter. The
female is less buff than the
streaked finches.

♂

White
moustache
and collar

Reed Bunting

Emberiza schoeniclus   15cm/6"
Habitat: Bogs, marshes, lakeside vegetation, bracken, fields in winter.
When seen: All year round.
Breeds: Nests in a tussock or on the ground. 2 broods. 4-5 eggs.
Voice: Low, full *seu, tseep*. Short, hesitant, dull song – *tsiptsiptsipchititik* etc.
Feeding: Seeds and insects taken on or near the ground.
Flight: Low and flitting with loosely flicked tail; weaker than that of finches.

Dark spot in
centre of breast
is often visible

Large
pale
bill

Lacks
pattern
on wings
and tail
(see Skylark)

*Corn Buntings are
often seen on wires,
fence posts and tops of
thin hedges*

'Blank'
facial
appearance

Tail lacks white

*Pale, buff-
brown plumage
with dark streaks*

Large, bulky bird, bigger
than other buntings and
finches, with little plumage
variation, but neatly
patterned when seen
closely.

Corn Bunting

Emberiza calandra   18cm/7"
Habitat: Dry, wide-open fields of corn, grassland, downs, coastal scrub.
When seen: All year round.
Breeds: A well-hidden nest low down in vegetation. 3-5 eggs.
Voice: Sharp *quit, tlip*. Song, from perched bird, is a monotonous, dry, stuttering
ticking, accelerating to a thin, rising trill – *tik tik tik tikikiktree-ee-ee*.
Feeding: Insects and seeds taken from the ground, not in trees.
Flight: Rather weak, heavy whirring action low over the ground.

Flies low, then swoops up onto perch with spread wings

White rump is especially distinctive on retreating bird

Note blue wing flash in flight

Jay flying into a dense oakwood; these birds are often seen feeding on acorns in October/November

Black, white and blue wings

Black tail

Streaked black and white crest

Black moustache

A highly distinctive, wary bird with broad wings. Can often be located by its calls. Only the *Hoopoe* is at all similar, but its crest, curved bill and wing pattern are quite different from the Jay's.

Body is pinkish with soft, velvety plumage

Continental birds are greyer than British birds

Jay

Garrulus glandarius   34cm/13½"

Habitat: Woodland of all kinds, parks.

When seen: All year round.

Breeds: Builds a twig nest in a tree. 5-6 eggs.

Voice: Varied nasal and whirring noises but typically a loud, screeching *skrairk*, *skairr*, etc. often heard from the depths of woods, where bird is concealed.

Feeding: Takes eggs, fruit, worms, beetles, grubs, nuts, etc. from trees or open ground. Leaps heavily about trees, tugging at acorns etc. Has a strong, leaping hop.

Flight: Highly characteristic heavy, jerky action with broad, round wings.

Long, slender
tail

White on
primaries
shows only
in flight

Tail is shorter
than adult's

Very young
JUVENILE

Magpies are often seen in pairs or small
parties, and are especially gregarious in
spring, gathering in trees or hedges.

White belly
and scapular
patch contrast
with black elsewhere

Iridescent colours of
tail are visible at
close range

White
scapular
patch

An unmistakeable black
and white bird with short,
rounded wings and a long
slender tail. Has a bold
walk or hop on the
ground.

Magpie

Pica pica 46cm/18"
Habitat: Thickets, open woodland, heaths, farmland, roadsides.
When seen: All year round.
Breeds: Large stick nest is roofed over, in a hedge or tree. 5-7 eggs.
Voice: Harsh, rattling chatter *chak-ak-ak-ak-ak-ak* etc.
Feeding: A bold and aggressive feeder, taking insects, rodents, eggs, scraps, seeds, etc.
from the ground or amongst trees and bushes.
Flight: Slow and laboured with quick wing action; weak, flapping flight with
intermittent glides.

Smaller head than
Carrion Crow
or Rook

Wings are more
narrow than
Carrion Crow's
or Rook's, and
wing-tips are
less fingered

Flight action is
quicker than Rook's
or Carrion Crow's

Struts about on ground, pausing
frequently to probe or look around

Jackdaws may form acrobatic flocks
above their roosts

Plumage is blackish,
with a dull grey sheen;
looks paler in sunlight

Black cap contrasts
with grey nape
(see Hooded Crow)

Distinctive
white eye

A small black and grey
crow – compare with
Carrion Crow and *Rook*.
Forms large flocks in the
tops of woodland trees, in
fields, on cliffs.

Jackdaw

Corvus monedula   33cm/13"
Habitat: Town parks, old buildings, woods, cliffs, fields and large lawns.
When seen: All year round.
Breeds: Builds a stick nest in a hole in a tree, cliff or building. 4-6 eggs.
Voice: A twanging *chack*, *kyaa*, etc., loud and emphatic, with a more musical, ringing
effect than that of other crows.
Feeding: Takes eggs, small bird chicks, worms, slugs, insects, etc. with quick, bold
actions, mostly from the ground.
Flight: Faster, more pigeon-like than that of the larger crows.

Wings are less angular than Carrion Crow's and taper to a more pointed tip

Tail is longer than Carrion Crow's and is rounded or wedge-shaped (see Raven)

Juvenile has all-black face, so may be confused with Carrion Crow – however, bill is more pointed than Crow's

Rooks nest and roost in tree-top colonies; large flocks are often seen at the rookery and elsewhere

JUVENILE

Peaked head

Bare, whitish face

Slender, pointed bill

Black plumage with blue and purple gloss

Baggy thigh feathers

A large black crow, regularly seen in large flocks. Its baggy thighs, slimmer bill and more peaked head distinguish it from the *Carrion Crow*. Unlike the *Raven*, it is not found on crags or sea cliffs.

Rook

Corvus frugilegus   46cm/18"
Habitat: Mixed farmland with woods, copses. tall trees.
When seen: All year round.
Breeds: Builds large nests in tree-top colonies. 4-6 eggs.
Voice: A pleasant mixture of deep *caw, kaah* notes, etc. with some higher, metallic calls – *kruk, tonk.*
Feeding: Typically, loosely scattered flocks roam fields in search of worms, insect larvae, etc. walking or occasionally hopping about and probing after food.
Flight: Regular, slower than Jackdaw's but smoother than Crow's; irregular flocks.

Carrion and Hooded Crows have a similar flight silhouette, but their colouring differs

CARRION

HOODED

Wings are squarer than Rook's, and tail is shorter, more square-tipped

Distinctive grey underparts

Carrion Crow flying to its nest in a tall tree in early spring

CARRION CROW (ENGLAND, WALES & S.SCOTLAND)

Squarer head and stout bill distinguish Carrion Crow from juvenile Rook

All-black plumage

HOODED CROW (N.SCOTLAND & IRELAND)

Pale grey or pinkish-grey body contrasts with black elsewhere

A single species with two distinct forms. They are the same size and shape, and both differ from the *Rook* in having a larger, flatter head, stouter bill and neat, tightly feathered thighs.

Carrion and Hooded Crows

Corvus corone 47cm/18½"
Habitat: All kinds of open country, moorland, crags, derelict land, seashores.
When seen: All year round; Hooded is also a winter visitor to eastern England.
Breeds: Solitary nests in trees (or bushes in hilly areas). 4-6 eggs.
Voice: Harsher than Rook's – *karr karr karr, cor*, etc. and higher *kreer kreer kreer*.
Feeding: Takes most food from the ground; walks or hops and picks for scraps, grain, seeds, worms, eggs, carrion, etc.
Flight: Strong and direct; slower action than Rook and rather less flexible.

Protruding head and neck

Long, angular wings

Broad, wedge- or diamond-shaped tail (see Rook)

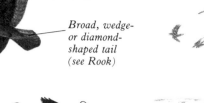

In flight, Raven rolls onto its back, then turns the right way up again (this incomplete roll is diagnostic)

Parties of Ravens gather over crags and perform aerial manoeuvres including steep dives, stoops and rolls

Long, arched, powerful bill (see Crow)

On the ground, birds may adopt sleek appearance; head and neck feathers may also be raised, giving a big-headed look

Shaggy 'beard' may be extended or smoothly flattened

An all-black bird, like the Carrion Crow, but much bigger and longer-winged, with a bigger head and bill, and more powerful and acrobatic flight.

Powerful legs

Broad tail (juvenile's is shorter)

Moulting adults in summer often have ragged wings

Raven

Corvus corax   64cm/25"
Habitat: Mountains, coastal cliffs, moors, extensive woods.
When seen: All year round.
Breeds: Builds a bulky stick nest in a tree or on a cliff ledge. 4-6 eggs.
Voice: Calls are loud and mostly deep, throaty and powerful – *prruk prruk*, *grok*, etc. Also a metallic, clanging *tonk*, *toktoktok*. Bold and noisy near the nest.
Feeding: Forages for all kinds of carrion, eggs, worms, etc. often in groups.
Flight: Powerful, masterly, impressive. Diagnostic roll; stoops and twisting dives; soars and glides well. Direct flight is stronger than Crow's.

Useful Addresses

There are many local bird clubs and natural history societies up and down the country which you could join in order to improve your birdwatching. Details of such clubs are available from the Royal Society for the Protection of Birds (RSPB). Members of the RSPB are welcomed by any of over 150 Members' Groups, which produce a programme of indoor meetings, film shows, coach outings, etc., and usually a series of bulletins or newsletters. Local bird reports are produced by most regional bird clubs and are extremely useful for finding out more on the species in your area.

The RSPB issue free to members a quarterly magazine — *Birds.* The Young Ornithologists' Club, at the same address as the RSPB, caters for birdwatchers under 15 and issues its own magazine, *Bird Life.* For information about membership, write to:

The Royal Society for the Protection of Birds,
The Lodge,
Sandy,
Bedfordshire.

The birdwatchers' own monthly magazine is *British Birds,* which is a mixture of authoritative papers on all aspects of birds and birdwatching, readers' notes, letters, reviews, recent news, up-to-date bird reports, photographs and drawings. Members of the RSPB can obtain *British Birds* at a reduced rate. The magazine is available on subscription from:

BB Circulation,
Fountains,
Park Lane,
Blunham,
Bedfordshire.

The Birdwatchers' Code

1. The welfare of the birds must come first.
2. Habitat must be protected.
3. Keep disturbance to birds and their habitats to a minimum.
4. When you find a rare bird think carefully about whom you should tell.
5. Do not harass rare migrants.
6. Abide by the Bird Protection Acts at all times.
7. Respect the rights of landowners.
8. Respect the rights of other people in the countryside.
9. Make your records available to the local bird recorder.
10. Behave abroad as you would when birdwatching at home.

This code has been drafted after consultation between the British Ornithologists' Union, the British Trust for Ornithology, the RSPB, the Scottish Ornithologists' Club, the Wildfowl Trust and the editors of *British Birds.*

Index of English Names

Page numbers referring to illustrations appear in **bold type**

Avocet **48**

Blackbird 94, **95**, 96, 97
Blackcap 99, **100**, 101, 109
Brambling **114**
Bullfinch 114, **115**
Bunting, Corn **119**
  Reed **119**
Buzzard 61, **62**, 63, 64

Chaffinch **114**, 115
Chiffchaff **102**, 103
Coot **28**, 29
Cormorant **8**, 9
Crow, Carrion 58, **77**, 122, 123, **124**, 125
  Hooded 122, **124**, 125
Cuckoo **75**
Curlew 45, **46**

Dipper **33**
Dove, Collared **74**
  Rock **73**
  Stock **72**
  Turtle **74**
Duck, Tufted 19, **22**, 23
Dunlin 39, **40**, 41
Dunnock 75, **88**

Eagle, Golden 62, **63**
Eider **21**

Fieldfare **98**
Firecrest **111**
Flycatcher, Pied 103, **105**
  Spotted 103, **105**
Fulmar **53**

Gadwall **16**
Gannet **11**
Garganey **17**
Godwit, Bar-tailed 41, 43, **45**, 46
  Black-tailed 43, **45**, 46
Goldcrest **111**
Goldeneye **23**
Goldfinch **116**
Goosander 23, 24, **25**, 26
Goose, Barnacle **13**
  Brent **13**
  Canada **13**
  Greylag **14**
  Pink-footed 14, **15**
  White-fronted **15**

Goshawk 60, **61**
Grebe, Great Crested 23, **26**
  Little **27**
Greenfinch **113**, 114, 116, 117
Greenshank **43**
Grouse, Red **68**
Guillemot **10**
Gull, Black-headed **49**
  Common 50, **51**
  Great Black-backed 11, **52**
  Herring **50**, 51, 52
  Lesser Black-backed **52**

Harrier, Hen **59**
  Marsh **59**
Heron, Grey **31**
Hobby **58**
Hoopoe 120

Jackdaw **122**, 123
Jay **120**

Kestrel **56**, 57, 58, 60, 75
Kingfisher **32**
Kittiwake **51**
Knot **41**

Lapwing **36**
Lark, Crested **85**, 86
Linnet **116**, 117

Magpie **121**
Mallard **16**, 17, 18, 20, 21, 24, 25
Martin, House **80**, 81, **82**, 83
  Sand **80**, 83
Merganser, Red-breasted **25**
Merlin **57**, 60
Moorhen 28, **29**, 30

Nightingale **99**, 100
Nuthatch **79**

Osprey **64**
Owl, Barn **65**, 66
  Little **65**
  Long-eared 66, **67**
  Short-eared 66, **67**
  Tawny **66**, 67
Oystercatcher 39, **46**, **48**

Partridge, Grey 68, **69**, 70
  Red-legged **69**
Peregrine **58**, 61
Pheasant **70**
Pigeon, Feral 72, **73**
Pintail 17, **21**
Pipit, Meadow 75, 84, **86**, 87
  Rock **87**
  Tree 84, **87**
Plover, Golden **37**
  Grey **37**
  Little Ringed **38**
  Ringed **38**
Pochard **19**, 22
Puffin, **11**, 52

Rail, Water **30**
Raven 58, 123, **125**
Razorbill **10**
Redpoll, Lesser 116, **117**
  Mealy 116, **117**
Redshank **43**, 45
Redstart **91**
  Black **91**
Redwing **98**
Robin 75, **90**, 91, 99, 105
Rook 122, **123**, 124, 125
Ruff 43, **44**

Sanderling 40, **41**
Sandpiper, Common **42**
Scaup **22**
Shag 8, **9**
Shelduck 20, **24**
Shoveler **20**
Siskin **117**
Skylark **84**, 85, 86, 87,119
Snipe 43, **47**
Sparrow, House **112**, 114
  Tree **112**, 114
Sparrowhawk **60**, 61, 75
Starling **94**, 95
Stonechat **92**
Swallow **80**, **81**, 82, 83
Swan, Bewick's **12**
  Mute **12**
  Whooper **12**
Swift **80**, 81, 82

Teal **17**, 18, 19
Tern, Arctic **54**
  Common **54**
  Little **55**

Sandwich **55**
Thrush, Mistle 57, 84, **97**, 98
  Song 84, 95, **96**, 97, 98
Tit, Blue **106**, **107**, 108, 109
  Coal **108**, 109
  Great **107**, 108
  Long-tailed **110**
  Marsh 100, 108, **109**
  Willow 108, **109**
Treecreeper **79**
Turnstone **39**

Wagtail, Grey **35**
  Pied **34**, 35, 75
  White **34**
  Yellow **35**
Warbler, Garden **99**, 100
  Reed 75, **104**
  Sedge **104**
  Willow **102**, 103
  Wood **103**
Wheatear **93**
Whimbrel **46**
Whinchat **92**, 93
Whitethroat **101**
  Lesser **101**
Wigeon 17, **18**, 19
Woodcock **47**
Woodlark **85**, 86
Woodpecker, Black **77**
  Great Spotted **78**
  Green 61, **76**, 78, 79
  Lesser Spotted **78**, 79
Woodpigeon **71**, 72
Wren 88, **89**, 111

Yellowhammer **118**

Index of Scientific Names

Page numbers referring to illustrations appear in **bold type**

Acanthis cannabina **116**, 117
 flammea 116, **117**
Accipiter gentilis 60, **61**
 nisus **60**, 61, 75
Acrocephalus
 schoenobaenus 104
 scirpaceus 75, **104**
Actitis hypoleucos 42
Aegithalos caudatus 110
Alauda arvensis **84**, 85, 86, 87, 119
Alca torda **10**
Alcedo atthis **32**
Alectoris rufa **69**
Anas acuta 17, **21**
 clypeata **20**
 crecca **17**, 18, 19
 penelope 17, **18**, 19
 platyrhynchos **16**, 17, 18, 20, 21, 24, 25
 querquedula **17**
 strepera **16**
Anser albifrons **15**
 anser **14**
 brachyrhynchus 14, **15**
Anthus pratensis 75, 84, **86**, 87
 spinoletta **87**
 trivialis 84, **87**
Apus apus **80**, 81, 82
Aquila chrysaetos 62, **63**
Ardea cinerea **31**
Arenaria interpres **39**
Asio flammeus 66, **67**
 otus 66, **67**
Athene noctua **65**
Aythya ferina **19**, 22
 fuligula 19, **22**, 23
 marila **22**

Branta bernicla **13**
 canadensis **13**
 leucopsis **13**
Bucephala clangula **23**
Buteo buteo 61, **62**, 63, 64

Calidris alba 40, **41**
 alpina 39, **40**, 41
 canutus **41**
Carduelis carduelis **116**
 chloris **113**, 114, 116, 117
 spinus **117**
Certhia familiaris **79**

Charadrius dubius **38**
 hiaticula **38**
Cinclus cinclus **33**
Circus aeruginosus **59**
 cyaneus **59**
Columba livia 72, **73**
 oenas **72**
 palumbus **71**, 72
Corvus corax 58, 123, **125**
 corone cornix 122, **124**, 125
 corone corone 58, **77**, 122, 123, **124**, 125
 frugilegus 122, **123**, 124, 125
 monedula **122**, 123
Cuculus canorus **75**
Cygnus columbianus **12**
 cygnus **12**
 olor **12**

Delichon urbica **80**, 81, **82**, 83
Dendrocopos major **78**
 minor **78**, 79
Dryocopus martius **77**

Emberiza calandra **119**
 citrinella **118**
 schoeniclus **119**
Erithacus rubecula 75, **90**, 91, 99, 105

Falco columbarius **57**, 60
 peregrinus **58**, 61
 subbuteo **58**
 tinnunculus **56**, 57, 58, 60, 75
Ficedula hypoleuca 103, **105**
Fratercula arctica **11**, 52
Fringilla coelebs **114**, 115
 montifringilla **114**
Fulica atra **28**, 29
Fulmarus glacialis **53**

Galerida cristata **85**, 86
Gallinago gallinago 43, **47**
Gallinula chloropus 28, **29**, 30
Garrulus glandarius **120**

Haematopus ostralegus 39, **46**, **48**
Hirundo rustica **80**, **81**, **82**,

Lagopus lagopus scoticus **68**
Larus argentatus **50**, 51, 52
 canus 50, **51**
 fuscus **52**
 marinus 11, **52**
 ridibundus **49**
Limosa lapponica 41, 43, **45**, 46
 limosa 43, **45**, 46
Lullula arborea **85**, 86
Luscinia megarhynchos **99**, 100

Mergus merganser 23, 24, **25**, 26
 serrator **25**
Motacilla alba **34**, 35, 75
 cinerea **35**
 flava **35**
Muscicapa striata 103, **105**

Numenius arquata 45, 46
 phaeopus 46

Oenanthe oenanthe **93**

Pandion haliaetus **64**
Parus ater 108, 109
 caeruleus **106**, **107**, 108, 109
 major **107**, 108
 montanus 108, **109**
 palustris 100, 108, **109**
Passer domesticus **112**, 114
 montanus **112**, 114
Perdix perdix 68, **69**, 70
Phalacrocorax aristotelis 8, **9**
 carbo **8**, 9
Phasianus colchicus **70**
Philomachus pugnax 43, **44**
Phoenicurus ochruros **91**
 phoenicurus **91**
Phylloscopus collybita **102**, 103
 sibilatrix **103**
 trochilus **102**, 103
Pica pica **121**
Picus viridis 61, **76**, 78, 79
Pluvialis apricaria **37**
 squatarola **37**
Podiceps cristatus 23, **26**

Prunella modularis 75, **88**
Pyrrhula pyrrhula 114, **115**

Rallus aquaticus **30**
Recurvirostra avosetta **48**
Regulus ignicapillus **111**
 regulus **111**
Riparia riparia **80**, **83**
Rissa tridactyla **51**

Saxicola rubetra **92**, 93
 torquata **92**
Scolopax rusticola **47**
Sitta europaea **79**
Somateria mollissima **21**
Sterna hirundo **54**
 minuta **54**
 paradisaea **54**
 sandvicensis **55**
Streptopelia decaocto **74**
 turtur **74**
Strix aluco **66**, 67
Sturnus vulgaris **94**, 95
Sula bassana **11**
Sylvia atricapilla 99, **100**, 101, 109
 borin **99**, 100
 communis **101**
 curruca **101**

Tachybaptus ruficollis **27**
Tadorna tadorna 20, **24**
Tringa nebularia **43**
 totanus **43**, 45
Troglodytes troglodytes 88, **89**, 111
Turdus iliacus **98**
 merula 94, **95**, 96, 97
 philomelos 84, 95, **96**, 97, 98
 pilaris **98**
 viscivorus 57, 84, **97**, 98
Tyto alba **65**, 66

Upupa epops 120
Uria aalge **10**

Vanellus vanellus **36**